D Read

SIDNEY

A Defence of Poetry

EDITED WITH AN INTRODUCTION

AND NOTES

BY

JAN VAN DORSTEN

Reader in English Literature
University of Leiden

a Ciceronian oration (with
digressions)

Cicero in Orator
3" offices"
conc
1. doc_____ form, instruct
→ pr
2. delecta_____ to please
→ tempered (middle) style

OXFORD UNIVERSITY PRESS

3. movere, flectere — to move or
"bend"
→ ornate (high) style

Oxford University Press, Ely House, London W. 1

GLASGOW NEW YORK TORONTO MELBOURNE WELLINGTON
CAPE TOWN IBADAN NAIROBI DAR ES SALAAM LUSAKA ADDIS ABABA
DELHI BOMBAY CALCUTTA MADRAS KARACHI LAHORE DACCA
KUALA LUMPUR SINGAPORE HONG KONG TOKYO

First published 1966
Reprinted 1971, 1973 (with corrections), 1975

Printed in Great Britain
at the University Press, Oxford
by Vivian Ridler
Printer to the University

ACKNOWLEDGEMENTS

I AM obliged to Viscount De L'Isle, V.C., for permission to consult, and quote from, the only known manuscript copy of Sidney's *Defence*.

I also wish to thank Miss Jean Robertson (Mrs. J. S. Brom-ley) for her guidance in textual matters and her advice on general principles; and my Leiden colleague, Mr. Michael Thorpe, for his comments on the introduction and notes.

CONTENTS

SIDNEY, LIFE AND WORKS—

John Dudley, Duke of Northumberland

John, Earl of Warwick	Lord Guildford Dudley = Lady Jane Grey	Robert, 1st Earl of Leicester

Mary = Sir Henry Sidney

1   2   3

Mary = Henry Herbert, Earl of Pembroke	Robert, 2nd Earl of Leicester

1553 Mary Tudor succeeds to the throne.
1554 12 Feb., Lady Jane Grey and her husband executed.
1554 25 July, Queen Mary marries Philip, King of Spain.

PHILIP SIDNEY, named after King Philip of Spain, born at Penshurst, 29 Nov. 1554

1557 'Tottel's "Miscellany"' printed.
1558 Death of Mary Tudor. Elizabeth succeeds to the throne.

With his life-long friend Fulke Greville enters Shrewsbury School

1564 Birth of Shakespeare and Marlowe. Death of Calvin.

Goes to Christ Church, Oxford

1568 Revolt of the Netherlands. Spenser's earliest work published
1569 anonymously in Van der Noot's *Theatre.*

Sets out on his 'Grand Tour'. Is made a Gentleman of the Chamber by the French King, 9 Aug.

1572 24 Aug., Massacre of St. Bartholomew.

Leaves Paris after the Massacre, travels to Heidelberg and Frankfort where he meets his self-appointed tutor Hubert Languet. Proceeds to Vienna, Hungary, and Italy

1573 Walsingham made Secretary of State.

Returns to England via Vienna, Poland, and the Low Countries; is introduced at Court. Sir Henry Sidney third time Lord Deputy of Ireland 1575

1576 First public theatre built near London.

Is sent on a diplomatic mission into Germany. Investigates the chances of a political alliance of Protestant states. Meets William of Orange on his journey back 1577

6

A CHRONOLOGICAL OUTLINE

Writes an entertainment, *The Lady of May* (pr 1598), for the Queen's visit to Leicester's house at Wanstead. Begins his *Arcadia*

1578 Lyly's *Euphues* published.

Writes to Queen Elizabeth opposing her intended marriage with Anjou. Completes first version of his *Arcadia*

1579 Spenser's *Shepherds' Calendar* (dedicated to Sidney) published.

Stephen Gosson, School of Abuse dedicated to Sidney Lodge – Reply to Gosson

Possible date of composition of his *Defence of Poetry*

1580 Drake completes his voyage round the world. *Sp started FQ*

Member of Parliament. Penelope Devereux, the 'Stella' of his poems, marries Lord Rich.

1581 Death of Languet. Northern Netherlands abjure the King of Spain.

Escorts Anjou to the Netherlands. Writes *Astrophil and Stella*

1582 Anjou arrives in the Netherlands.

Knighted. Marries Frances, Sir Francis Walsingham's daughter

1583

Revises *Arcadia*. Writes *Defence of the Earl of Leicester*

1584 Death of Anjou. William of Orange assassinated.

Begins translating Mornay's *De la Verité de la Religion Chrétienne*. Begins translation of the *Psalms*, to be continued by his sister. Prepares to sail to the West Indies with Drake. Appointed Governor of Flushing

1585 Treaty of Nonsuch. Leicester's expedition to the Netherlands.

Travels in the northern Netherlands. Is actively involved in politics. Wounded in a skirmish near Zutphen. Dies at Arnhem, 27 Oct.

1586 Leicester proclaimed Governor-General of the United Provinces.

Buried with great ceremony in St. Paul's, 16 Feb. *The Trueness of the Christian Religion*, completed by Arthur Golding, published

1587 Execution of Mary Queen of Scots. End of Leicester's régime in the Netherlands.

1589 Puttenham Arte of English Poesie

1588 Death of Leicester. Armada.

Revised *Arcadia* first published

1590 Death of Walsingham. First three books of *Fairy Queen* published.

Astrophil and Stella first published Old *Arcadia* III–V first published (in 1st folio edition)

1591

1593 Death of Marlowe. Shakespeare's first publication, *Venus and Adonis*. *1594 Rape of Lucrece*

Defence of Poetry first published *Arcadia* published 'with sundry new additions'

1595

1598 Death of King Philip II of Spain.

7

INTRODUCTION

IN AN AGE of remarkable personalities, Sir Philip Sidney held a unique place. Artists and scholars sought his advice and dedicated their works to this '*Rendez-vous* of Learning', although he was neither a Maecenas nor particularly powerful. The impact of his mind was felt by explorers, politicians, and theologians, but he cannot be held responsible for any famous discovery, treaty, or conference. It is clear that his significance should be measured not only by his achievements, but especially by the quality of his example.

He left behind an impressive *œuvre*—much of it unfinished, none intended for immediate publication—which on his deathbed he desired to be destroyed. Posterity, while disregarding these instructions, has observed without effort his last words 'love my memory'; and it has looked upon the immortal phrase 'thy necessity is yet greater than mine' (which he, himself fatally injured, is said to have spoken when offering his water-bottle to a dying soldier) as an epitome of his generous nature.

Though young, he served the world for an *exemplum* of true nobility. His own writings show him to have been accomplished without pedantry or professionalism, and possessing in a rare degree the gift of modesty. His manners were charming, but his convictions unwavering; he was both loyal and ambitious, deeply conscious of his responsibilities as a Christian knight, and thoughtfully witty in his speech; and he impressed his contemporaries by a happy balance of merits, rather than a mere accumulation of them. They recognized in him the ideals of their age; but his memory continued to be loved long after that, because he still represented the 'life and action good and great' (as one of his friends termed it) to which he had always applied his talents.

It is no longer necessary to defend the *Defence* by pointing out that 'this noble little treatise well deserves more attention', as did the preface to the O.U.P. edition of 1907. Sidney's essay, always admired as a brilliant performance, is now firmly established as a landmark in English literary history and read everywhere as a key to Elizabethan poetry.

If persuasion is one of the aims of all verbal arts, his 'defence' was written to achieve precisely that. Sidney observed the compositional rules for this type of oratory, moving from *exordium* to *narratio*, making his *propositio*, next examining, then refuting, the charges against 'the accused', finally delivering a superlatively eloquent *peroratio*, swaying the evidence convincingly in favour of his client Poetry so that we, the Jury, cannot but unanimously find him 'not guilty'. Within this traditional framework he applied a careful mixture of impassioned rhetoric and almost casual understatement, wit, and seriousness, his renowned 'irony'; and although the oration was never meant to be pronounced, the speech-rhythms, the involved sentences full of interjections and repetitions, and some effectively imperfect constructions, create an authentic tone of almost *extempore* oral delivery.

As a treatise on poetry, the *Defence* is theoretical rather than critical in the modern sense of the word. Most of the ideas expressed in it are not original thoughts, but represent Sidney's selections from the countless theories and literary commonplaces with which any self-respecting sixteenth-century humanist was familiar. Thus they are a summary of what *his* milieu believed poetry to be; while at the same time the number of comparable statements made by others is so great that a really full commentary on sources and background would totally obscure the issue and always remain incomplete. Its significance lies in the manner in which current trends in European art theory were first made generally available in England, and in the English language, at a time when Shakespeare's generation was about to give that country its spectacular lead in the world of letters. Of continental descent but undeniably British in application, the *Defence* was the more authoritative because its writer was a known scholar-patron, a favourite courtier, and himself a prominent experimental poet.

Sidney's treatise illustrates how an Elizabethan could look at literature. It contains interesting remarks on all 'kinds' of poetry (with special reference to one or two individual works), and it has some famous pages on English as a literary language. But perhaps the most remarkable part is the 'narration', in which the nature of poetry is defined. Sidney argues that the art which teaches most efficiently what is good and true and which most induces man to act accordingly must needs be the greatest human art; and that poetry can do this better than man's traditional tutors, philosophy and history. For the historian is tied to the particular events of the past which do not necessarily possess any general validity, while the philosopher, who has a reputation for being dull or difficult, frightens away the very public he ought to reach. Poetry, having neither disadvantage, is moreover uniquely capable of enriching the mind and furthering judicious action because it translates general concepts of truth into specific images and examples, which 'speaking pictures' the memory, aided by the ornaments of verse, can retain without difficulty: thus they lie ready for use, in perfect order, whenever a man may need them in actual life. It follows that the poet's responsibilities are great. Sidney rejects firmly the common notion that all literary inspiration originates in a 'divine frenzy', the authors themselves being little more than well-tuned instruments. Instead he declares—with an unmistakably Puritan emphasis on the responsible individual mind—that making poetry is, essentially, the discipline of an enlightened intellect, which seeks to overcome earth-bound thoughts and inclinations in an attempt to recover something of the true and perfect knowledge lost since 'the first accursed Fall'. The poet's task, therefore, though called 'imitation', is not to represent this world as it is seen by our imperfect eyes, but to 'figure forth' a 'nature' of a higher order, re-creating in his imaginative mind the world as it may have existed in the Creator's mind.

This doctrine, ambitious and humble at the same time, is not only crucial to an understanding of Sidney's life and writings, but also indicates how poetry could cease to be regarded as a mere rhetorical art. In the *Defence*, the limitless scope of poetry was defined in terms such as no Englishman had ventured to use before.

The treatise, first published nine years after its author's death but known to have circulated in manuscript, enjoyed great popularity. Like the *Arcadia*, it was frequently reprinted and translated.

The text of this edition[1] is the first to be based upon a critical comparison of the unique manuscript copy (Penshurst Place, MS. De L'Isle no. 1226), the quarto edition *The Defence of Poesie*, printed for William Ponsonby in 1595 (from which all folio editions—1598–1674—derive), and the independently printed quarto *An Apologie for Poetrie*, published by Henry Olney in the same year.

[1] For a discussion of editorial procedure, see *Miscellaneous Prose of Sir Philip Sidney* (O.U.P.—in preparation), which edition will also include a full critical apparatus and more elaborate annotations.

Since Sidney's essay is a 'Defence' rather than an 'Apology' in the modern sense of the word, and because the actual defence part is concerned not only with 'poesy' (the art of making poems) but also with the general product 'poetry', the title *A Defence of Poetry*, as given in the Penshurst MS., is chosen for this new edition. Sidney himself, moreover, uses the phrase in his introduction (18.8; cf. 47.16).

Spelling and punctuation have been normalized. The notes aim at offering a minimum amount of explanatory information.

SELECT BIBLIOGRAPHY

I. Editions

The Complete Works of Sir Philip Sidney, ed. A. Feuillerat, 4 vols., Cambridge, 1912–26. Old-spelling texts.

The Poems of Sir Philip Sidney, ed. W. A. Ringler, Oxford, 1962. Old-spelling edition. Valuable notes and introduction.

An Apology for Poetry, ed. G. Shepherd, London, 1965. Modernized text. Various useful notes and comments.

II. Biography and Criticism

J. Buxton, *Sir Philip Sidney and the English Renaissance*, 2nd ed., London, 1964.

Fulke Greville, Baron Brooke, *The Life of the Renowned Sir Philip Sidney*, 1652, ed. N. Smith, Oxford, 1907.

D. Kalstone, *Sidney's Poetry, Contexts and Interpretations*, Cambridge Mass., 1965.

K. O. Myrick, *Sir Philip Sidney as a Literary Craftsman*, Cambridge Mass., 1935.

M. W. Wallace, *The Life of Sir Philip Sidney*, London, 1915.

A DEFENCE OF POETRY—
THE ARGUMENT

[handwritten annotations:] hevoic / lyric / tragic / comic / satiric / iambic / elegiac / pastoral **confirmatio**

15

A DEFENCE OF POETRY

WHEN THE right virtuous Edward Wotton and I were at
the Emperor's court together, we gave ourselves to learn
horsemanship of John Pietro Pugliano, one that with great
commendation had the place of an esquire in his stable.
And he, according to the fertileness of the Italian wit, did 5
not only afford us the demonstration of his practice, but
sought to enrich our minds with the contemplations
therein, which he thought most precious. But with none I
remember mine ears were at that time more laden, than
when (either angered with slow payment, or moved with 10
our learner-like admiration) he exercised his speech in the
praise of his faculty. He said soldiers were the noblest estate
of mankind, and horsemen the noblest of soldiers. He said
they were the masters of war and ornaments of peace,
speedy goers and strong abiders, triumphers both in camps 15
and courts. Nay, to so unbelieved a point he proceeded as
that no earthly thing bred such wonder to a prince as to
be a good horseman—skill of government was but a
pedanteria in comparison. Then would he add certain
praises, by telling what a peerless beast the horse was, the 20
only serviceable courtier without flattery, the beast of most
beauty, faithfulness, courage, and such more, that if I had
not been a piece of a logician before I came to him, I think
he would have persuaded me to have wished myself a
horse. But thus much at least with his no few words he 25
drave into me, that self-love is better than any gilding to
make that seem gorgeous wherein ourselves be parties.
Wherein, if Pugliano's strong affection and weak arguments will not satisfy you, I will give you a nearer example

arms
argument
cf Courtier
Bk I

17

of myself, who (I know not by what mischance) in these my
not old years and idlest times having slipped into the title
of a poet, am provoked to say something unto you in the
defence of that my unelected vocation, which if I handle
5 with more good will than good reasons, bear with me,
since the scholar is to be pardoned that followeth the steps
of his master. And yet I must say that, as I have more just
cause to make a pitiful defence of poor poetry, which
from almost the highest estimation of learning is fallen to
10 be the laughing-stock of children, so have I need to bring
some more available proofs: since the former is by no
man barred of his deserved credit, the silly latter hath had
even the names of philosophers used to the defacing of it,
with great danger of civil war among the Muses.

[NARRATION
WHAT POETRY IS
precedes all other
learnings]   And first, truly, to all them that, professing learning,
inveigh against poetry may justly be objected that they go
very near to ungratefulness, to seek to deface that which,
in the noblest nations and languages that are known, hath
been the first light-giver to ignorance, and first nurse,
20 whose milk by little and little enabled them to feed afterwards of tougher knowledges. And will they now play
the hedgehog that, being received into the den, drave out
his host? Or rather the vipers, that with their birth kill their
parents?

25   Let learned Greece in any of his manifold sciences be
able to show me one book before Musaeus, Homer, and
Hesiod, all three nothing else but poets. Nay, let any history
be brought that can say any writers were there before them,
if they were not men of the same skill, as Orpheus, Linus,
30 and some other are named, who, having been the first
of that country that made pens deliverers of their knowledge to the posterity, may justly challenge to be called

their fathers in learning: for not only in time they had
this priority (although in itself antiquity be venerable) but
went before them, as causes to draw with their charming
sweetness the wild untamed wits to an admiration of
knowledge. So, as Amphion was said to move stones with   5
his poetry to build Thebes, and Orpheus to be listened to
by beasts—indeed stony and beastly people—so among the
Romans were Livius Andronicus and Ennius. So in the
Italian language the first that made it aspire to be a treasure-
house of science were the poets Dante, Boccaccio, and   10
Petrarch. So in our English were Gower and Chaucer,
after whom, encouraged and delighted with their excellent
fore-going, others have followed, to beautify our mother
tongue, as well in the same kind as in other arts.

   This did so notably show itself, that the philosophers of   15
Greece durst not a long time appear to the world but under
the masks of poets. So Thales, Empedocles, and Parmenides
sang their natural philosophy in verses; so did Pythagoras
and Phocylides their moral counsels; so did Tyrtaeus in
war matters, and Solon in matters of policy: or rather they,   20
being poets, did exercise their delightful vein in those
points of highest knowledge, which before them lay hid
to the world. For that wise Solon was directly a poet it is
manifest, having written in verse the notable fable of the
Atlantic Island, which was continued by Plato. And truly   25
even Plato whosoever well considereth shall find that in
the body of his work, though the inside and strength were
philosophy, the skin, as it were, and beauty depended
most of poetry: for all standeth upon dialogues, wherein he
feigneth many honest burgesses of Athens to speak of such   30
matters, that, if they had been set on the rack, they would
never have confessed them, besides his poetical describing
the circumstances of their meetings, as the well ordering

of a banquet, the delicacy of a walk, with interlacing mere
tales, as Gyges' ring and others, which who knoweth not
to be flowers of poetry did never walk into Apollo's
garden.

5   And even historiographers (although their lips sound of
things done, and verity be written in their foreheads) have
been glad to borrow both fashion and, perchance, weight
of the poets. So Herodotus entitled his History by the
name of the nine Muses; and both he and all the rest that
10 followed him either stale or usurped of poetry their
passionate describing of passions, the many particularities
of battles, which no man could affirm; or, if that be denied
me, long orations put in the mouths of great kings and
captains, which it is certain they never pronounced.

15   So that truly neither philosopher nor historiographer
could at the first have entered into the gates of popular
judgements, if they had not taken a great passport of poetry,
which in all nations at this day where learning flourisheth
not, is plain to be seen; in all which they have some feeling
20 of poetry.

In Turkey, besides their law-giving divines, they have
no other writers but poets. In our neighbour country
Ireland, where truly learning goeth very bare, yet are their
poets held in a devout reverence. Even among the most
25 barbarous and simple Indians where no writing is, yet have
they their poets who make and sing songs, which they call
areytos, both of their ancestors' deeds and praises of their
gods: a sufficient probability that, if ever learning come
among them, it must be by having their hard dull wits
30 softened and sharpened with the sweet delights of poetry—
for until they find a pleasure in the exercises of the mind,
great promises of much knowledge will little persuade
them that know not the fruits of knowledge. In Wales,

the true remnant of the ancient Britons, as there are good authorities to show the long time they had poets, which they called bards, so through all the conquests of Romans, Saxons, Danes, and Normans, some of whom did seek to ruin all memory of learning from among them, yet do 5 their poets even to this day last; so as it is not more notable in soon beginning than in long continuing.

But since the authors of most of our sciences were the Romans, and before them the Greeks, let us a little stand upon their authorities, but even so far as to see what names 10 they have given unto this now scorned skill.

Among the Romans a poet was called *vates*, which is as [poet-prophet] much as a diviner, foreseer, or prophet, as by his conjoined words *vaticinium* and *vaticinari* is manifest: so heavenly a title did that excellent people bestow upon this heart- 15 ravishing knowledge. And so far were they carried into the admiration thereof, that they thought in the chanceable hitting upon any such verses great foretokens of their following fortunes were placed. Whereupon grew the word of *Sortes Virgilianae*, when by sudden opening 20 Virgil's book they lighted upon any verse of his making, whereof the histories of the emperors' lives are full: as of Albinus, the governor of our island, who in his childhood met with this verse

     Arma amens capio nec sat rationis in armis   25

Frantic I seize arms: yet little purpose is there in arms. Aeneid

and in his age performed it. Which, although it were a very vain and godless superstition, as also it was to think spirits were commanded by such verses—whereupon this word charms, derived of *carmina*, cometh—so yet serveth it to show the great reverence those wits were held in; and 30 altogether not without ground, since both the oracles of Delphos and Sibylla's prophecies were wholly delivered in verses. For that same exquisite observing of number and measure in the words, and that high flying liberty of conceit proper to the poet, did seem to have some divine force in it.

5   And may not I presume a little further, to show the reasonableness of this word *vates*, and say that the holy David's Psalms are a divine poem? If I do, I shall not do it without the testimony of great learned men, both ancient and modern. But even the name of Psalms will speak for me, which being interpreted, is nothing but songs; then that it is fully written in metre, as all learned hebricians agree, although the rules be not yet fully found; lastly and principally, his handling his prophecy, which is merely poetical: for what else is the awaking his musical instruments, the often and free changing of persons, his notable *prosopopœias*, when he maketh you, as it were, see God coming in His majesty, his telling of the beasts' joyfulness and hills leaping, but a heavenly poesy, wherein almost he showeth himself a passionate lover of that unspeakable and everlasting beauty to be seen by the eyes of the mind, only cleared by faith? But truly now having named him, I fear me I seem to profane that holy name, applying it to poetry, which is among us thrown down to so ridiculous an estimation. But they that with quiet judgements will look a little deeper into it, shall find the end and working of it such as, being rightly applied, deserveth not to be scourged out of the Church of God.

But now let us see how the Greeks named it, and how they deemed of it. The Greeks called him a 'poet', which name hath, as the most excellent, gone through other languages. It cometh of this word ποιεῖν, which is, to make: wherein, I know not whether by luck or wisdom, we Englishmen have met with the Greeks in calling him a maker: which name, how high and incomparable a title it is, I had rather were known by marking the scope of other sciences than by any partial allegation.

There is no art delivered to mankind that hath not the [art and nature] works of nature for his principal object, without which they could not consist, and on which they so depend, as they become actors and players, as it were, of what nature will have set forth. So doth the astronomer look upon the stars, and, by that he seeth, set down what order nature 10 hath taken therein. So doth the geometrician and arithmetician in their diverse sorts of quantities. So doth the musicians in time tell you which by nature agree, which not. The natural philosopher thereon hath his name, and the moral philosopher standeth upon the natural virtues, 15 vices, or passions of man; and follow nature (saith he) therein, and thou shalt not err. The lawyer saith what men have determined; the historian what men have done. The grammarian speaketh only of the rules of speech; and the rhetorician and logician, considering what in nature will 20 soonest prove and persuade, thereon give artificial rules, which still are compassed within the circle of a question according to the proposed matter. The physician weigheth the nature of man's body, and the nature of things helpful or hurtful unto it. And the metaphysic, though it be in the 25 second and abstract notions, and therefore be counted supernatural, yet doth he indeed build upon the depth of nature. Only the poet, disdaining to be tied to any such subjection, lifted up with the vigour of his own invention, doth grow in effect another nature, in making things either 30 better than nature bringeth forth, or, quite anew, forms such as never were in nature, as the Heroes, Demigods, Cyclops, Chimeras, Furies, and such like: so as he goeth

hand in hand with nature, not enclosed within the narrow
warrant of her gifts, but freely ranging only within the
zodiac of his own wit. Nature never set forth the earth in
so rich tapestry as divers poets have done; neither with so
5 pleasant rivers, fruitful trees, sweet-smelling flowers, nor
whatsoever else may make the too much loved earth more
lovely. Her world is brazen, the poets only deliver a golden.

But let those things alone, and go to man—for whom as
the other things are, so it seemeth in him her uttermost
10 cunning is employed—and know whether she have brought
forth so true a lover as Theagenes, so constant a friend as
Pylades, so valiant a man as Orlando, so right a prince as
Xenophon's Cyrus, so excellent a man every way as
Virgil's Aeneas. Neither let this be jestingly conceived,
15 because the works of the one be essential, the other in
imitation or fiction; for any understanding knoweth the
skill of each artificer standeth in that *idea* or fore-conceit
of the work, and not in the work itself. And that the poet
hath that *idea* is manifest, by delivering them forth in
20 such excellency as he had imagined them. Which delivering
forth also is not wholly imaginative, as we are wont to say
by them that build castles in the air; but so far substantially
it worketh, not only to make a Cyrus, which had been but
a particular excellency as nature might have done, but to
25 bestow a Cyrus upon the world to make many Cyruses, if
they will learn aright why and how that maker made him.

Neither let it be deemed too saucy a comparison to
balance the highest point of man's wit with the efficacy of
nature; but rather give right honour to the heavenly
30 Maker of that maker, who having made man to His own
likeness, set him beyond and over all the works of that
second nature: which in nothing he showeth so much as in
poetry, when with the force of a divine breath he bringeth

things forth surpassing her doings—with no small arguments to the credulous of that first accursed fall of Adam, since our erected wit maketh us know what perfection is, and yet our infected will keepeth us from reaching unto it. But these arguments will by few be understood, and by fewer granted. This much (I hope) will be given me, that the Greeks with some probability of reason gave him the name above all names of learning.

Now let us go to a more ordinary opening of him, that the truth may be the more palpable: and so I hope, though we get not so unmatched a praise as the etymology of his names will grant, yet his very description, which no man will deny, shall not justly be barred from a principal commendation.

Poesy therefore is an art of imitation, for so Aristotle termeth it in the word μίμησις—that is to say, a representing, counterfeiting, or figuring forth—to speak metaphorically, a speaking picture—with this end, to teach and delight.

[PROPOSITION: A DEFINITION OF POESY]

Of this have been three general kinds. The chief, both in antiquity and excellency, were they that did imitate the unconceivable excellencies of God. Such were David in his Psalms; Solomon in his Song of Songs, in his Ecclesiastes, and Proverbs; Moses and Deborah in their Hymns; and the writer of Job: which, beside other, the learned Emanuel Tremellius and Franciscus Junius do entitle the poetical part of the Scripture. Against these none will speak that hath the Holy Ghost in due holy reverence. (In this kind, though in a full wrong divinity, were Orpheus, Amphion, Homer in his Hymns, and many other, both Greeks and Romans.) And this poesy must be used by

[DIVISIONS
I. THREE KINDS OF POETRY
i. divine poetry]

whosoever will follow St. James's counsel in singing psalms when they are merry, and I know is used with the fruit of comfort by some, when, in sorrowful pangs of their death-bringing sins, they find the consolation of the
5 never-leaving goodness.

[ii. philosophical poetry etc.]

The second kind is of them that deal with matters philosophical, either moral, as Tyrtaeus, Phocylides, Cato, or natural, as Lucretius and Virgil's *Georgics;* or astronomical, as Manilius and Pontanus; or historical, as Lucan: which
10 who mislike, the fault is in their judgement quite out of taste, and not in the sweet food of sweetly uttered knowledge.

[iii. poetry strictly speaking]

But because this second sort is wrapped within the fold of the proposed subject, and takes not the course of his own
15 invention, whether they properly be poets or no let grammarians dispute, and go to the third, indeed right poets, of whom chiefly this question ariseth: betwixt whom and these second is such a kind of difference as betwixt the meaner sort of painters, who counterfeit only
20 such faces as are set before them, and the more excellent, who having no law but wit, bestow that in colours upon you which is fittest for the eye to see: as the constant though lamenting look of Lucretia, when she punished in herself another's fault, wherein he painteth not Lucretia
25 whom he never saw, but painteth the outward beauty of such a virtue. For these third be they which most properly do imitate to teach and delight, and to imitate borrow nothing of what is, hath been, or shall be; but range, only reined with learned discretion, into the divine considera-

What may be & what should be

30 tion of what may be and should be. These be they that, as the first and most noble sort may justly be termed *vates,* so these are waited on in the excellentest languages and best understandings with the fore-described name of

poets. For these indeed do merely make to imitate, and imitate both to delight and teach; and delight, to move men to take that goodness in hand, which without delight they would fly as from a stranger; and teach, to make them know that goodness whereunto they are moved— which being the noblest scope to which ever any learning was directed, yet want there not idle tongues to bark at them.

These be subdivided into sundry more special denomina- tions. The most notable be the heroic, lyric, tragic, comic, satiric, iambic, elegiac, pastoral, and certain others, some of these being termed according to the matter they deal with, some by the sorts of verses they liked best to write in; for indeed the greatest part of poets have apparelled their poetical inventions in that numbrous kind of writing which is called verse—indeed but apparelled, verse being but an ornament and no cause to poetry, since there have been many most excellent poets that never versified, and now swarm many versifiers that need never answer to the name of poets. For Xenophon, who did imitate so excellently as to give us *effigiem iusti imperii*, the portraiture of a just empire, under the name of Cyrus, (as Cicero saith of him) made therein an absolute heroical poem. So did Heliodorus in his sugared invention of that picture of love in Theagenes and Chariclea; and yet both these wrote in prose: which I speak to show that it is not rhyming and versing that maketh a poet—no more than a long gown maketh an advocate, who though he pleaded in armour should be an advocate and no soldier. But it is that feigning notable images of virtues, vices, or what else, with that delightful teaching, which must be the right describing note to know a poet by; although indeed the senate of poets hath chosen verse as their fittest raiment, meaning,

[2. SUBDIVISION: eight 'parts']

as in matter they passed all in all, so in manner to go beyond
them: not speaking (table-talk fashion or like men in a
dream) words as they chanceably fall from the mouth, but
peising each syllable of each word by just proportion
5 according to the dignity of the subject.

[EXAMINATION
1]
Now therefore it shall not be amiss first to weigh this
latter sort of poetry by his works, and then by his parts;
and if in neither of these anatomies he be condemnable, I
hope we shall obtain a more favourable sentence.

[PURSUIT OF
LEARNING]
This purifying of wit—this enriching of memory,
enabling of judgement, and enlarging of conceit—which
commonly we call learning, under what name soever it
come forth, or to what immediate end soever it be directed,
the final end is to lead and draw us to as high a perfection
15 as our degenerate souls, made worse by their clayey
lodgings, can be capable of.

This, according to the inclination of the man, bred many-
formed impressions. For some that thought this felicity
principally to be gotten by knowledge, and no knowledge
20 to be so high or heavenly as acquaintance with the stars,
gave themselves to astronomy; others, persuading themselves to be demigods if they knew the causes of things,
became natural and supernatural philosophers; some an
admirable delight drew to music; and some the certainty
25 of demonstration to the mathematics. But all, one and
other, having this scope: to know, and by knowledge to
lift up the mind from the dungeon of the body to the
enjoying his own divine essence.

But when by the balance of experience it was found that
30 the astronomer, looking to the stars, might fall in a ditch,
that the inquiring philosopher might be blind in himself,
and the mathematician might draw forth a straight line

with a crooked heart, then lo, did proof, the overruler
of opinions, make manifest that all these are but serving
sciences, which, as they have each a private end in themselves, so yet are they all directed to the highest end of the
mistress-knowledge, by the Greeks called ἀρχιτεκτονική, 5
which stands (as I think) in the knowledge of a man's self,
in the ethic and politic consideration, with the end of well-
doing and not of well-knowing only—even as the saddler's
next end is to make a good saddle, but his further end to
serve a nobler faculty, which is horsemanship, so the horse- 10
man's to soldiery, and the soldier not only to have the skill,
but to perform the practice of a soldier. So that, the
ending end of all earthly learning being virtuous action,
those skills that most serve to bring forth that have a most
just title to be princes over all the rest.   15

   Wherein, if we can, show we the poet's nobleness, by
setting him before his other competitors. Among whom
as principal challengers step forth the moral philosophers,
whom, me thinketh, I see coming towards me with a
sullen gravity, as though they could not abide vice by 20
daylight, rudely clothed for to witness outwardly their
contempt of outward things, with books in their hands
against glory, whereto they set their names, sophistically
speaking against subtlety, and angry with any man in
whom they see the foul fault of anger. These men casting 25
largess as they go, of definitions, divisions, and distinctions,
with a scornful interrogative do soberly ask whether it
be possible to find any path so ready to lead a man to virtue
as that which teacheth what virtue is; and teach it not
only by delivering forth his very being, his causes and 30
effects, but also by making known his enemy, vice, which
must be destroyed, and his cumbersome servant, passion,
which must be mastered; by showing the generalities that

containeth it, and the specialities that are derived from it; lastly, by plain setting down how it extendeth itself out of the limits of a man's own little world to the government of families and maintaining of public societies.

[history]   The historian scarcely giveth leisure to the moralist to say so much, but that he, laden with old mouse-eaten records, authorizing himself (for the most part) upon other histories, whose greatest authorities are built upon the notable foundation of hearsay; having much ado to accord

10 differing writers and to pick truth out of their partiality; better acquainted with a thousand years ago than with the present age, and yet better knowing how this world goeth than how his own wit runneth; curious for antiquities and inquisitive of novelties; a wonder to young folks and a

15 tyrant in table talk, denieth, in a great chafe, that any man for teaching of virtue, and virtuous actions is comparable to him. 'I am *testis temporum, lux veritatis, vita memoriae, magistra vitae, nuntia vetustatis.* The philosopher', saith he, 'teacheth a disputative virtue, but I do an active. His virtue

20 is excellent in the dangerless Academy of Plato, but mine showeth forth her honourable face in the battles of Marathon, Pharsalia, Poitiers, and Agincourt. He teacheth virtue by certain abstract considerations, but I only bid you follow the footing of them that have gone before you.

25 Old-aged experience goeth beyond the fine-witted philosopher, but I give the experience of many ages. Lastly, if he make the songbook, I put the learner's hand to the lute; and if he be the guide, I am the light.' Then would he allege you innumerable examples, confirming

30 story by stories, how much the wisest senators and princes have been directed by the credit of history, as Brutus, Alphonsus of Aragon, and who not, if need be? At length the long line of their disputation maketh a point in this,

patterning a commonwealth was most absolute, in
perchance hath not so absolutely performed n
question is, whether the feigned image of poetry o
ular instruction of philosophy hath the more forc
ching: wherein if the philosophers have more right
wed themselves philosophers than the poets have
ained to the high top of their profession, as in truth

> Mediocribus esse poetis,
> Non dii, non homines, non concessere columnae;

is, I say again, not the fault of the art, but that by few men
hat art can be accomplished.

Certainly, even our Saviour Christ could as well have
given the moral commonplaces of uncharitableness and
humbleness as the divine narration of Dives and Lazarus;
or of disobedience and mercy, as that heavenly discourse
of the lost child and the gracious father; but that His
through-searching wisdom knew the estate of Dives
burning in hell, and of Lazarus in Abraham's bosom,
would more constantly (as it were) inhabit both the memory and judgement. Truly, for myself, meseems I see before mine eyes the lost child's disdainful prodigality, turned
to envy a swine's dinner: which by the learned divines
are thought not historical acts, but instructing parables.

For conclusion, I say the philosopher teacheth, but he
teacheth obscurely, so as the learned only can understand
him, that is to say, he teacheth them that are already
taught; but the poet is the food for the tenderest stomachs,
the poet is indeed the right popular philosopher, whereof
Aesop's tales give good proof: whose pretty allegories,
stealing under the formal tales of beasts, make many, more
beastly than beasts, begin to hear the sound of virtue from
these dumb speakers.

that the one giveth the precept, and the other the
example.

Now whom shall we find (since the question standeth
for the highest form in the school of learning) to be moderator? Truly, as me seemeth, the poet; and if not a moderator, 5
even the man that ought to carry the title from them
both, and much more from all other serving sciences.
Therefore compare we the poet with the historian and with
the moral philosopher; and if he go beyond them both,
no other human skill can match him. For as for the divine, 10
with all reverence it is ever to be excepted, not only for
having his scope as far beyond any of these as eternity
exceedeth a moment, but even for passing each of these in
themselves. And for the lawyer, though *Ius* be the daughter
of Justice, and justice the chief of virtues, yet because he 15
seeketh to make men good rather *formidine poenae* than
virtutis amore; or, to say righter, doth not endeavour to
make men good, but that their evil hurt not others; having
no care, so he be a good citizen, how bad a man he be:
therefore as our wickedness maketh him necessary, and 20
necessity maketh him honourable, so is he not in the deepest
truth to stand in rank with these who all endeavour to
take naughtiness away and plant goodness even in the
secretest cabinet of our souls. And these four are all that
any way deal in that consideration of men's manners, 25
which being the supreme knowledge, they that best breed
it deserve the best commendation.

The philosopher, therefore, and the historian are they
which would win the goal, the one by precept, the other
by example. But both, not having both, do both halt. For 30
the philosopher, setting down with thorny arguments the
bare rule, is so hard of utterance and so misty to be conceived, that one that hath no other guide but him shall

[poetry and philosophy]

makes the abstract concrete

their means are different?

wade in him till he be old before he shall find sufficient
cause to be honest. For his knowledge standeth so upon
the abstract and general, that happy is that man who may
understand him, and more happy that can apply what he
5 doth understand. On the other side, the historian, wanting
the precept, is so tied, not to what should be but to what is,
to the particular truth of things and not to the general
reason of things, that his example draweth no necessary
consequence, and therefore a less fruitful doctrine.

10   Now doth the peerless poet perform both: for whatsoever the philosopher saith should be done, he giveth a
perfect picture of it in someone by whom he presupposeth
it was done, so as he coupleth the general notion with the
particular example. A perfect picture I say, for he yieldeth
15 to the powers of the mind an image of that whereof the
philosopher bestoweth but a wordish description, which
doth neither strike, pierce, nor possess the sight of the soul
so much as that other doth. For as in outward things, to a
man that had never seen an elephant or a rhinoceros,
20 who should tell him most exquisitely all their shapes,
colour, bigness, and particular marks, or of a gorgeous
palace, an *architector*, with declaring the full beauties,
might well make the hearer able to repeat, as it were by
rote, all he had heard, yet should never satisfy his inward
25 conceit with being witness to itself of a true lively knowledge; but the same man, as soon as he might see those
beasts well painted, or the house well in model, should
straightways grow, without need of any description, to a
judicial comprehending of them: so no doubt the philoso-
30 pher with his learned definitions—be it of virtue, vices,
matters of public policy or private government—re-
plenisheth the memory with many infallible grounds of
wisdom, which, notwithstanding, lie dark before the

aginative and judging pow
ated or figured forth by the sp
     Tully taketh much pains, an
poetical helps, to make us kno
country hath in us. Let us but h
in the midst of Troy's flames, or
of all Calypso's delights bewail
and beggarly Ithaca. Anger, the
madness: let but Sophocles bring
killing or whipping sheep and ox
army of Greeks, with their chief
Menelaus, and tell me if you hav
insight into anger than finding in th
and difference. See whether wisdo
Ulysses and Diomedes, valour in A
Nisus and Euryalus, even to an ignor
apparent shining; and, contrarily, the r
in Oedipus, the soon repenting pride
self-devouring cruelty in his father Atr
ambition in the two Theban brothers,
of revenge in Medea; and, to fall lov
Gnatho and our Chaucer's Pandar so
now use their names to signify their trad
virtues, vices, and passions so in their
laid to the view, that we seem not to h
clearly to see through them.

     But even in the most excellent determi
ness, what philosopher's counsel can so
prince, as the feigned Cyrus in Xenophon
man in all fortunes, as Aeneas in Virgi
commonwealth, as the way of Sir Thomas
I say the way, because where Sir Thomas
was the fault of the man and not of the poet

But now may it be alleged that if this imagining of [poetry and
matters be so fit for the imagination, then must the historian history]
needs surpass, who bringeth you images of true matters,
such as indeed were done, and not such as fantastically or
falsely may be suggested to have been done. Truly, 5
Aristotle himself, in his discourse of poesy, plainly deter-
mineth this question, saying that poetry is φιλοσοφώτερον
and σπουδαιότερον, that is to say, it is more philosophical
and more studiously serious than history. His reason is,
because poesy dealeth with καθόλου, that is to say, with the 10
universal consideration, and the history with καθέκαστον,
the particular: now, saith he, the universal weighs what
is fit to be said or done, either in likelihood or necessity
(which the poesy considereth in his imposed names), and
the particular only marks whether Alcibiades did, or 15
suffered, this or that. Thus far Aristotle: which reason of
his (as all his) is most full of reason. For indeed, if the
question were whether it were better to have a particular
act truly or falsely set down, there is no doubt which is
to be chosen, no more than whether you had rather have 20
Vespasian's picture right as he was, or, at the painter's
pleasure, nothing resembling. But if the question be for
your own use and learning, whether it be better to have it
set down as it should be, or as it was, then certainly is
more doctrinable the feigned Cyrus in Xenophon than the 25
true Cyrus in Justin, and the feigned Aeneas in Virgil
than the right Aeneas in Dares Phrygius: as to a lady that
desired to fashion her countenance to the best grace, a
painter should more benefit her to portrait a most sweet
face, writing Canidia upon it, than to paint Canidia as she 30
was, who, Horace sweareth, was full ill-favoured.

If the poet do his part aright, he will show you in Tantalus, Atreus, and such like, nothing that is not to be shunned;

in Cyrus, Aeneas, Ulysses, each thing to be followed; where the historian, bound to tell things as things were, cannot be liberal (without he will be poetical) of a perfect pattern, but, as in Alexander or Scipio himself, show doings, some to be liked, some to be misliked. And then how will you discern what to follow but by your own discretion, which you had without reading Quintus Curtius? And whereas a man may say, though in universal consideration of doctrine the poet prevaileth, yet that the history, in his saying such a thing was done, doth warrant a man more in that he shall follow—the answer is manifest: that, if he stand upon that was (as if he should argue, because it rained yesterday, therefore it should rain today), then indeed hath it some advantage to a gross conceit; but if he know an example only informs a conjectured likelihood, and so go by reason, the poet doth so far exceed him as he is to frame his example to that which is most reasonable (be it in warlike, politic, or private matters), where the historian in his bare *Was* hath many times that which we call fortune to overrule the best wisdom. Many times he must tell events whereof he can yield no cause; or, if he do, it must be poetically.

For that a feigned example hath as much force to teach as a true example (for as for to move, it is clear, since the feigned may be tuned to the highest key of passion), let us take one example wherein an historian and a poet did concur. Herodotus and Justin do both testify that Zopyrus, King Darius' faithful servant, seeing his master long resisted by the rebellious Babylonians, feigned himself in extreme disgrace of his king: for verifying of which, he caused his own nose and ears to be cut off, and so flying to the Babylonians, was received, and for his known valour so sure credited, that he did find means to deliver them over to

Darius. Much like matter doth Livy record of Tarquinius and his son. Xenophon excellently feigneth such another stratagem performed by Abradatas in Cyrus' behalf. Now would I fain know, if occasion be presented unto you to serve your prince by such an honest dissimulation, why you do not as well learn it of Xenophon's fiction as of the other's verity; and truly so much the better, as you shall save your nose by the bargain: for Abradatas did not counterfeit so far. So then the best of the historian is subject to the poet; for whatsoever action, or faction, whatsoever counsel, policy, or war stratagem the historian is bound to recite, that may the poet (if he list) with his imitation make his own, beautifying it both for further teaching, and more delighting, as it please him: having all, from Dante's heaven to his hell, under the authority of his pen. Which if I be asked what poets have done so, as I might well name some, so yet say I, and say again, I speak of the art, and not of the artificer.

Now, to that which commonly is attributed to the praise of history, in respect of the notable learning is got by marking the success, as though therein a man should see virtue exalted and vice punished—truly that commendation is particular to poetry, and far off from history. For indeed poetry ever sets virtue so out in her best colours, making Fortune her well-waiting handmaid, that one must needs be enamoured of her. Well may you see Ulysses in a storm, and in other hard plights; but they are but exercises of patience and magnanimity, to make them shine the more in the near-following prosperity. And of the contrary part, if evil men come to the stage, they ever go out (as the tragedy writer answered to one that misliked the show of such persons) so manacled as they little animate folks to follow them. But the history, being captived to the truth

of a foolish world, is many times a terror from well-doing, and an encouragement to unbridled wickedness. For see we not valiant Miltiades rot in his fetters? The just Phocion and the accomplished Socrates put to death like traitors?
5 The cruel Severus live prosperously? The excellent Severus miserably murdered? Sulla and Marius dying in their beds? Pompey and Cicero slain then when they would have thought exile a happiness? See we not virtuous Cato driven to kill himself, and rebel Caesar so
10 advanced that his name yet, after 1600 years, lasteth in the highest honour? And mark but even Caesar's own words of the aforenamed Sulla (who in that only did honestly, to put down his dishonest tyranny), *literas nescivit*, as if want of learning caused him to do well. He meant it not by poetry,
15 which, not content with earthly plagues, deviseth new punishments in hell for tyrants, nor yet by philosophy, which teacheth *occidendos esse*; but no doubt by skill in history, for that indeed can afford you Cypselus, Periander, Phalaris, Dionysius, and I know not how many more of
20 the same kennel, that speed well enough in their abominable injustice of usurpation.

I conclude, therefore, that he excelleth history, not only in furnishing the mind with knowledge, but in setting it forward to that which deserveth to be called and accounted
25 good: which setting forward, and moving to well-doing, indeed setteth the laurel crown upon the poets as victorious, not only of the historian, but over the philosopher, howsoever in teaching it may be questionable.

['moving']   For suppose it be granted (that which I suppose with
30 great reason may be denied) that the philosopher, in respect of his methodical proceeding, doth teach more perfectly than the poet, yet do I think that no man is so

much φιλοφιλόσοφος as to compare the philosopher in moving with the poet. And that moving is of a higher degree than teaching, it may by this appear, that it is well nigh both the cause and effect of teaching. For who will be taught, if he be not moved with desire to be taught? And what so much good doth that teaching bring forth (I speak still of moral doctrine) as that it moveth one to do that which it doth teach? For, as Aristotle saith, it is not γνῶσις but πρᾶξις must be the fruit. And how πρᾶξις can be, without being moved to practise, it is no hard matter to consider.

The philosopher showeth you the way, he informeth you of the particularities, as well of the tediousness of the way, as of the pleasant lodging you shall have when your journey is ended, as of the many by-turnings that may divert you from your way. But this is to no man but to him that will read him, and read him with attentive studious painfulness; which constant desire whosoever hath in him, hath already passed half the hardness of the way, and therefore is beholding to the philosopher but for the other half. Nay truly, learned men have learnedly thought that where once reason hath so much overmastered passion as that the mind hath a free desire to do well, the inward light each mind hath in itself is as good as a philosopher's book; since in nature we know it is well to do well, and what is well, and what is evil, although not in the words of art which philosophers bestow upon us; for out of natural conceit the philosophers drew it. But to be moved to do that which we know, or to be moved with desire to know, *hoc opus, hic labor est*.

Now therein of all sciences (I speak still of human, and according to the human conceit) is our poet the monarch. For he doth not only show the way, but giveth so sweet a

prospect into the way, as will entice any man to enter into it. Nay, he doth, as if your journey should lie through a fair vineyard, at the first give you a cluster of grapes, that full of that taste, you may long to pass further. He beginneth
5 not with obscure definitions, which must blur the margin with interpretations, and load the memory with doubtfulness; but he cometh to you with words set in delightful proportion, either accompanied with, or prepared for, the well enchanting skill of music; and with a tale forsooth
10 he cometh unto you, with a tale which holdeth children from play, and old men from the chimney corner. And, pretending no more, doth intend the winning of the mind from wickedness to virtue—even as the child is often brought to take most wholesome things by hiding them
15 in such other as have a pleasant taste, which, if one should begin to tell them the nature of *aloes* or *rhabarbarum* they should receive, would sooner take their physic at their ears than at their mouth. So is it in men (most of which are childish in the best things, till they be cradled in their
20 graves): glad they will be to hear the tales of Hercules, Achilles, Cyrus, Aeneas; and, hearing them, must needs hear the right description of wisdom, valour, and justice; which, if they had been barely, that is to say philosophically, set out, they would swear they be brought
25 to school again.

That imitation whereof poetry is, hath the most conveniency to nature of all other, insomuch that, as Aristotle saith, those things which in themselves are horrible, as cruel battles, unnatural monsters, are made in poetical
30 imitation delightful. Truly, I have known men that even with reading *Amadis de Gaule* (which God knoweth wanteth much of a perfect poesy) have found their hearts moved to the exercise of courtesy, liberality, and especially

courage. Who readeth Aeneas carrying old Anchises on his back, that wisheth not it were his fortune to perform so excellent an act? Whom doth not these words of Turnus move, the tale of Turnus having planted his image in the imagination,   5

>   Fugientem haec terra videbit?
>   Usque adeone mori miserum est?

Where the philosophers, as they scorn to delight, so must they be content little to move—saving wrangling whether *virtus* be the chief or the only good, whether the contem-   10
plative or the active life do excell—which Plato and Boeth-ius well knew, and therefore made mistress Philosophy very often borrow the masking raiment of poesy. For even those hard-hearted evil men who think virtue a school name, and know no other good but *indulgere genio*, and   15
therefore despise the austere admonitions of the philoso-pher, and feel not the inward reason they stand upon, yet will be content to be delighted—which is all the good-fellow poet seemeth to promise—and so steal to see the form of goodness (which seen they cannot but love) ere   20
themselves be aware, as if they took a medicine of cherries.

  Infinite proofs of the strange effects of this poetical invention might be alleged; only two shall serve, which are so often remembered as I think all men know them. The one of Menenius Agrippa, who, when the whole   25
people of Rome had resolutely divided themselves from the senate, with apparent show of utter ruin, though he were (for that time) an excellent orator, came not among them upon trust of figurative speeches or cunning insinua-tions, and much less with far-fet maxims of philosophy,   30
which (especially if they were Platonic) they must have learned geometry before they could well have conceived; but forsooth he behaves himself like a homely and familiar

poet. He telleth them a tale, that there was a time when all
the parts of the body made a mutinous conspiracy against
the belly, which they thought devoured the fruits of each
other's labour; they concluded they would let so unprofit-
5 able a spender starve. In the end, to be short (for the tale is
notorious, and as notorious that it was a tale), with
punishing the belly they plagued themselves. This applied
by him wrought such effect in the people, as I never read
that only words brought forth but then so sudden and so
10 good an alteration; for upon reasonable conditions a
perfect reconcilement ensued. The other is of Nathan the
prophet, who, when the holy David had so far forsaken
God as to confirm adultery with murder, when he was
to do the tenderest office of a friend in laying his own shame
15 before his eyes, sent by God to call again so chosen a
servant, how doth he it but by telling of a man whose
beloved lamb was ungratefully taken from his bosom: the
application most divinely true, but the discourse itself
feigned; which made David (I speak of the second and
20 instrumental cause) as in a glass see his own filthiness, as
that heavenly psalm of mercy well testifieth.

By these, therefore, examples and reasons, I think it may
be manifest that the poet, with that same hand of delight,
doth draw the mind more effectually than any other art
25 doth. And so a conclusion not unfitly ensue: that, as
virtue is the most excellent resting place for all worldly
learning to make his end of, so poetry, being the most
familiar to teach it, and most princely to move towards it,
in the most excellent work is the most excellent workman.

[EXAMINATION 2 THE 'PARTS' OF POETRY] But I am content not only to decipher him by his works
(although works, in commendation or dispraise, must ever
hold a high authority), but more narrowly will examine

his parts; so that (as in a man) though all together may carry a presence full of majesty and beauty, perchance in some one defectuous piece we may find blemish.

Now in his parts, kinds, or species (as you list to term them), it is to be noted that some poesies have coupled together two or three kinds, as the tragical and comical, whereupon is risen the tragi-comical. Some, in the manner, have mingled prose and verse, as Sannazzaro and Boethius. Some have mingled matters heroical and pastoral. But that cometh all to one in this question, for, if severed they be good, the conjunction cannot be hurtful. Therefore, perchance forgetting some and leaving some as needless to be remembered, it shall not be amiss in a word to cite the special kinds, to see what faults may be found in the right use of them.

Is it then the Pastoral poem which is misliked? (For perchance where the hedge is lowest they will soonest leap over.) Is the poor pipe disdained, which sometime out of Meliboeus' mouth can show the misery of people under hard lords or ravening soldiers, and again, by Tityrus, what blessedness is derived to them that lie lowest from the goodness of them that sit highest; sometimes, under the pretty tales of wolves and sheep, can include the whole considerations of wrong-doing and patience; sometimes show that contentions for trifles can get but a trifling victory: where perchance a man may see that even Alexander and Darius, when they strave who should be cock of this world's dunghill, the benefit they got was that the after-livers may say

> Haec memini et victum frustra contendere Thirsin:
> Ex illo Corydon, Corydon est tempore nobis.

Or is it the lamenting Elegiac; which in a kind heart would move rather pity than blame; who bewails with the

pastoral

elegiac

great philosopher Heraclitus, the weakness of mankind and
the wretchedness of the world; who surely is to be praised,
either for compassionate accompanying just causes of
lamentations, or for rightly painting out how weak be the
passions of woefulness? Is it the bitter but wholesome
Iambic, who rubs the galled mind, in making shame the
trumpet of villainy, with bold and open crying out against
naughtiness? Or the Satiric, who

Iambic

satire

Omne vafer vitium ridenti tangit amico;

who sportingly never leaveth till he make a man laugh at
folly, and at length ashamed, to laugh at himself, which he
cannot avoid without avoiding the folly; who, while

circum praecordia ludit,

giveth us to feel how many headaches a passionate life
bringeth us to; how, when all is done,

Est Ulubris, animus si nos non deficit aequus?

comedy

No, perchance it is the Comic, whom naughty play-
makers and stage-keepers have justly made odious. To
the arguments of abuse I will answer after. Only this much
now is to be said, that the comedy is an imitation of the
common errors of our life, which he representeth in the
most ridiculous and scornful sort that may be, so as it is
impossible that any beholder can be content to be such a
one. Now, as in geometry the oblique must be known as
well as the right, and in arithmetic the odd as well as
the even, so in the actions of our life who seeth not the
filthiness of evil wanteth a great foil to perceive the beauty
of virtue. This doth the comedy handle so in our private
and domestical matters as with hearing it we get as it were
an experience what is to be looked for of a niggardly
Demea, of a crafty Davus, of a flattering Gnatho, of a

vainglorious Thraso; and not only to know what effects
are to be expected, but to know who be such, by the
signifying badge given them by the comedian. And little
reason hath any man to say that men learn the evil by seeing
it so set out, since, as I said before, there is no man living 5
but, by the force truth hath in nature, no sooner seeth
these men play their parts, but wisheth them *in pistrinum*;
although perchance the sack of his own faults lie so hidden
behind his back that he seeth not himself dance
the same measure; whereto yet nothing can more open 10
his eyes than to find his own actions contemptibly set
forth.

So that the right use of comedy will (I think) by nobody
be blamed; and much less of the high and excellent
Tragedy, that openeth the greatest wounds, and showeth 15
forth the ulcers that are covered with tissue; that maketh
kings fear to be tyrants, and tyrants manifest their tyrannical
humours; that, with stirring the affects of admiration and
commiseration, teacheth the uncertainty of this world,
and upon how weak foundations gilden roofs are builded; 20
that maketh us know

> Qui sceptra saevus duro imperio regit
> Timet timentes; metus in auctorem redit.

But how much it can move, Plutarch yieldeth a notable
testimony of the abominable tyrant Alexander Pheraeus, 25
from whose eyes a tragedy, well made and represented,
drew abundance of tears, who without all pity had
murdered infinite numbers, and some of his own blood:
so as he, that was not ashamed to make matters for tragedies,
yet could not resist the sweet violence of a tragedy. And 30
if it wrought no further good in him, it was that he, in
despite of himself, withdrew himself from hearkening to
that which might mollify his hardened heart. But it is not

the tragedy they do mislike; for it were too absurd to cast
out so excellent a representation of whatsoever is most
worthy to be learned.

Is it the Lyric that most displeaseth, who with his tuned
lyre and well-accorded voice, giveth praise, the reward of
virtue, to virtuous acts; who gives moral precepts, and
natural problems; who sometimes raiseth up his voice to
the height of the heavens, in singing the lauds of the immortal God? Certainly, I must confess my own barbarous-
ness, I never heard the old song of Percy and Douglas that
I found not my heart moved more than with a trumpet;
and yet is it sung but by some blind crowder, with no
rougher voice than rude style; which, being so evil
apparelled in the dust and cobwebs of that uncivil age,
what would it work trimmed in the gorgeous eloquence
of Pindar? In Hungary I have seen it the manner at all
feasts, and other such meetings, to have songs of their
ancestors' valour, which that right soldierlike nation think
one of the chiefest kindlers of brave courage. The incomparable Lacedemonians did not only carry that kind of
music ever with them to the field, but even at home, as
such songs were made, so were they all content to be
singers of them—when the lusty men were to tell what they
did, the old men what they had done, and the young
what they would do. And where a man may say that
Pindar many times praiseth highly victories of small
moment, matters rather of sport than virtue; as it may be
answered, it was the fault of the poet, and not of the
poetry, so indeed the chief fault was in the time and custom
of the Greeks, who set those toys at so high a price that
Philip of Macedon reckoned a horserace won at Olympus
among his three fearful felicities. But as the unimitable
Pindar often did, so is that kind most capable and most fit

to awake the thoughts from the sleep of idleness to embrace
honourable enterprises.

There rests the Heroical—whose very name (I think)
should daunt all backbiters: for by what conceit can a
tongue be directed to speak evil of that which draweth
with him no less champions than Achilles, Cyrus, Aeneas,
Turnus, Tydeus, and Rinaldo?—who doth not only
teach and move to a truth, but teacheth and moveth to
the most high and excellent truth; who maketh magnanimity and justice shine through all misty fearfulness and
foggy desires; who, if the saying of Plato and Tully be
true, that who could see virtue would be wonderfully
ravished with the love of her beauty—this man sets her
out to make her more lovely in her holiday apparel, to
the eye of any that will deign not to disdain until they
understand. But if anything be already said in the defence
of sweet poetry, all concurreth to the maintaining the
heroical, which is not only a kind, but the best and most
accomplished kind of poetry. For as the image of each
action stirreth and instructeth the mind, so the lofty image
of such worthies most inflameth the mind with desire to
be worthy, and informs with counsel how to be worthy.
Only let Aeneas be worn in the tablet of your memory,
how he governeth himself in the ruin of his country; in
the preserving his old father, and carrying away his religious ceremonies; in obeying God's commandment to leave
Dido, though not only all passionate kindness, but even
the human consideration of virtuous gratefulness, would
have craved other of him; how in storms, how in sports,
how in war, how in peace, how a fugitive, how victorious,
how besieged, how besieging, how to strangers, how to
allies, how to enemies, how to his own; lastly, how in his
inward self, and how in his outward government—and I

think, in a mind not prejudiced with a prejudicating humour, he will be found in excellency fruitful, yea, even as
Horace saith,

melius Chrysippo et Crantore.

5 But truly I imagine it falleth out with these poet-
whippers, as with some good women, who often are
sick, but in faith they cannot tell where; so the name of
poetry is odious to them, but neither his cause nor effects,
neither the sum that contains him, nor the particularities
10 descending from him, give any fast handle to their carping
dispraise.

[SUMMARY] Since then poetry is of all human learning the most
ancient and of most fatherly antiquity, as from whence
other learnings have taken their beginnings; since it is so
15 universal that no learned nation doth despise it, nor
barbarous nation is without it; since both Roman and
Greek gave such divine names unto it, the one of prophesy-
ing, the other of making, and that indeed that name of
making is fit for him, considering that where all other arts
20 retain themselves within their subject, and receive, as it
were, their being from it, the poet only bringeth his own
stuff, and doth not learn a conceit out of a matter, but
maketh matter for a conceit; since neither his description
nor end containing any evil, the thing described cannot be
25 evil; since his effects be so good as to teach goodness and to
delight the learners; since therein (namely in moral
doctrine, the chief of all knowledges) he doth not only far
pass the historian, but, for instructing, is well nigh comparable to the philosopher, for moving leaves him behind
30 him; since the Holy Scripture (wherein there is no unclean-
ness) hath whole parts in it poetical, and that even our
Saviour Christ vouchsafed to use the flowers of it; since

poetry considered separate from poets

all his kinds are not only in their united forms but in their
severed dissections fully commendable; I think (and think
I think rightly) the laurel crown appointed for triumphant
captains doth worthily (of all other learnings) honour the
poet's triumph.   5

But because we have ears as well as tongues, and that the [REFUTATION
lightest reasons that may be will seem to weigh greatly, if OF CHARGES
nothing be put in the counterbalance, let us hear, and, as AGAINST POETRY]
well as we can, ponder what objections be made against
this art, which may be worthy either of yielding or 10
answering.

First, truly I note not only in these μισόμουσοι, poet- [the critics]
haters, but in all that kind of people who seek a praise by
dispraising others, that they do prodigally spend a great
many wandering words in quips and scoffs, carping and 15
taunting at each thing which, by stirring the spleen, may
stay the brain from a through-beholding the worthiness
of the subject. Those kind of objections, as they are full of a
very idle easiness, since there is nothing of so sacred a
majesty but that an itching tongue may rub itself upon it, 20
so deserve they no other answer, but, instead of laughing
at the jest, to laugh at the jester. We know a playing wit can
praise the discretion of an ass, the comfortableness of
being in debt, and the jolly commodities of being sick of
the plague. So of the contrary side, if we will turn Ovid's 25
verse

Ut lateat virtus proximitate mali,

that good lie hid in nearness of the evil, Agrippa will be as
merry in showing the vanity of science as Erasmus was in
the commending of folly. Neither shall any man or matter 30
escape some touch of these smiling railers. But for Erasmus
and Agrippa, they had another foundation than the

superficial part would promise. Marry, these other pleasant faultfinders, who will correct the verb before they understand the noun, and confute others' knowledge before they confirm their own—I would have them only remember that scoffing cometh not of wisdom. So as the best title in true English they get with their merriments is to be called good fools; for so have our grave forefathers ever termed that humorous kind of jesters.

[verse]   But that which giveth greatest scope to their scorning humour is rhyming and versing. It is already said (and, as I think, truly said), it is not rhyming and versing that maketh poesy. One may be a poet without versing, and a versifier without poetry. But yet, presuppose it were inseparable (as indeed it seemeth Scaliger judgeth), truly it were an inseparable commendation. For if *oratio* next to *ratio*, speech next to reason, be the greatest gift bestowed upon mortality, that cannot be praiseless which doth most polish that blessing of speech; which considers each word, not only (as a man may say) by his most forcible quality, but by his best measured quantity, carrying even in themselves a harmony—without, perchance, number, measure, order, proportion be in our time grown odious. But lay aside the just praise it hath, by being the only fit speech for music (music, I say, the most divine striker of the senses), thus much is undoubtedly true, that if reading be foolish without remembering, memory being the only treasure of knowledge, those words which are fittest for memory are likewise most convenient for knowledge. Now, that verse far exceedeth prose in the knitting up of memory, the reason is manifest: the words (besides their delight, which hath a great affinity to memory) being so set as one cannot be lost but the whole work fails; which accusing itself, calleth the remembrance back to itself, and

so most strongly confirmeth it. Besides, one word so, as
it were, begetting another, as, be it in rhyme or measured
verse, by the former a man shall have a near guess to the
follower. Lastly, even they that have taught the art of
memory have showed nothing so apt for it as a certain   5
room divided into many places well and thoroughly
known. Now, that hath the verse in effect perfectly, every
word having his natural seat, which seat must needs make
the word remembered. But what needeth more in a thing
so known to all men? Who is it that ever was a scholar   10
that doth not carry away some verses of Virgil, Horace, or
Cato, which in his youth he learned, and even to his old
age serve him for hourly lessons? But the fitness it hath
for memory is notably proved by all delivery of arts:
wherein for the most part, from grammar to logic,   15
mathematics, physic, and the rest, the rules chiefly necessary to be borne away are compiled in verses. So that,
verse being in itself sweet and orderly, and being best for
memory, the only handle of knowledge, it must be in
jest that any man can speak against it.   20

    Now then go we to the most important imputations   [FOUR CHARGES]
laid to the poor poets. For aught I can yet learn, they are
these. First, that there being many other more fruitful
knowledges, a man might better spend his time in them
than in this. Secondly, that it is the mother of lies. Thirdly,   25
that it is the nurse of abuse, infecting us with many
pestilent desires; with a siren's sweetness drawing the
mind to the serpent's tail of sinful fancies (and herein,
especially, comedies give the largest field to ear, as Chaucer
saith); how, both in other nations and in ours, before poets   30
did soften us, we were full of courage, given to martial
exercises, the pillars of manlike liberty, and not lulled
asleep in shady idleness with poets' pastimes. And lastly,

and chiefly, they cry out with open mouth as if they had overshot Robin Hood, that Plato banished them out of his commonwealth. Truly, this is much, if there be much truth in it.

[i. poetry a waste of time]

First, to the first. That a man might better spend his time, is a reason indeed; but it doth (as they say) but *petere principium*. For if it be as I affirm, that no learning is so good as that which teacheth and moveth to virtue; and that none can both teach and move thereto so much as
10 poetry: then is the conclusion manifest that ink and paper cannot be to a more profitable purpose employed. And certainly, though a man should grant their first assumption, it should follow (methinks) very unwillingly, that good is not good, because better is better. But I still and utterly
15 deny that there is sprong out of earth a more fruitful knowledge.

[ii. poets are liars]

To the second, therefore, that they should be the principal liars, I answer paradoxically, but truly, I think truly, that of all writers under the sun the poet is the least liar,
20 and, though he would, as a poet can scarcely be a liar. The astronomer, with his cousin the geometrician, can hardly escape, when they take upon them to measure the height of the stars. How often, think you, do the physicians lie, when they aver things good for sicknesses, which
25 afterwards send Charon a great number of souls drowned in a potion before they come to his ferry? And no less of the rest, which take upon them to affirm. Now, for the poet, he nothing affirms, and therefore never lieth. For, as I take it, to lie is to affirm that to be true which is false.
30 So as the other artists, and especially the historian, affirming many things, can, in the cloudy knowledge of mankind, hardly escape from many lies. But the poet (as I said before) never affirmeth. The poet never maketh any circles about

politically important, I think

your imagination, to conjure you to believe for true what he writes. He citeth not authorities of other histories, but even for his entry calleth the sweet Muses to inspire into him a good invention; in truth, not labouring to tell you what is or is not, but what should or should not be. And therefore, though he recount things not true, yet because he telleth them not for true, he lieth not—without we will say that Nathan lied in his speech before-alleged to David; which as a wicked man durst scarce say, so think I none so simple would say that Aesop lied in the tales of his beasts; for who thinks that Aesop wrote it for actually true were well worthy to have his name chronicled among the beasts he writeth of. What child is there, that, coming to a play, and seeing *Thebes* written in great letters upon an old door, doth believe that it is Thebes? If then a man can arrive to that child's age to know that the poets' persons and doings are but pictures what should be, and not stories what have been, they will never give the lie to things not affirmatively but allegorically and figuratively written. And therefore, as in history, looking for truth, they may go away full fraught with falsehood, so in poesy, looking but for fiction, they shall use the narration but as an imaginative ground-plot of a profitable invention. But hereto is replied, that the poets give names to men they write of, which argueth a conceit of an actual truth, and so, not being true, proves a falsehood. And doth the lawyer lie then, when under the names of *John-a-stiles* and *John-a-nokes* he puts his case? But that is easily answered. Their naming of men is but to make their picture the more lively, and not to build any history: painting men, they cannot leave men nameless. We see we cannot play at chess but that we must give names to our chessmen; and yet, methinks, he were a very partial champion of truth that would say we lied for giving a piece of wood the reverend title of a bishop. The poet nameth Cyrus or Aeneas no other way than to show what men of their fames, fortunes, and estates should do.

[iii. poems are sinful fancies] Their third is, how much it abuseth men's wit, training it to wanton sinfulness and lustful love: for indeed that is the principal, if not only, abuse I can hear alleged. They say, the comedies rather teach than reprehend amorous conceits. They say the lyric is larded with passionate
10 sonnets; the elegiac weeps the want of his mistress; and that even to the heroical, Cupid hath ambitiously climbed. Alas, Love, I would thou couldst as well defend thyself as thou canst offend others. I would those on whom thou dost attend could either put thee away, or yield good
15 reason why they keep thee. But grant love of beauty to be a beastly fault (although it be very hard, since only man, and no beast, hath that gift to discern beauty); grant that lovely name of Love to deserve all hateful reproaches (although even some of my masters the philosophers spent a good
20 deal of their lamp-oil in setting forth the excellency of it); grant, I say, whatsoever they will have granted, that not only love, but lust, but vanity, but (if they list) scurrility, possesseth many leaves of the poets' books; yet think I, when this is granted, they will find their sentence may
25 with good manners put the last words foremost, and not say that poetry abuseth man's wit, but that man's wit abuseth poetry.

For I will not deny but that man's wit may make poesy, which should be εἰκαστική (which some learned have
30 defined: figuring forth good things), to be φανταστική (which doth, contrariwise, infect the fancy with unworthy objects), as the painter, that should give to the eye either some excellent perspective, or some fine picture, fit for

building or fortification, or containing in it some notable
example (as Abraham sacrificing his son Isaac, Judith
killing Holofernes, David fighting with Goliath), may
leave those, and please an ill-pleased eye with wanton
shows of better hidden matters. But what, shall the abuse
of a thing make the right use odious? Nay truly, though I
yield that poesy may not only be abused, but that being
abused, by the reason of his sweet charming force, it can
do more hurt than any other army of words: yet shall it
be so far from concluding that the abuse should give
reproach to the abused, that, contrariwise, it is a good
reason that whatsoever, being abused, doth most harm,
being rightly used (and upon the right use each thing
conceiveth his title), doth most good. Do we not see the
skill of physic, the best rampire to our often-assaulted
bodies, being abused, teach poison, the most violent
destroyer? Doth not knowledge of law, whose end is to
even and right all things, being abused, grow the crooked
fosterer of horrible injuries? Doth not (to go to the highest)
God's word abused breed heresy, and His name abused
become blasphemy? Truly, a needle cannot do much hurt,
and as truly (with leave of ladies be it spoken) it cannot do
much good: with a sword thou mayst kill thy father, and
with a sword thou mayst defend thy prince and country.
So that, as in their calling poets fathers of lies they said
nothing, so in this their argument of abuse they prove the
commendation.

They allege herewith, that before poets began to be in
price our nation had set their hearts' delight upon action,
and not imagination: rather doing things worthy to be
written, than writing things fit to be done. What that
before-time was, I think scarcely Sphinx can tell, since no
memory is so ancient that hath not the precedent of poetry.

And certain it is that, in our plainest homeliness, yet never was the Albion nation without poetry. Marry, this argument, though it be levelled against poetry, yet is it indeed a chainshot against all learning, or bookishness as they commonly term it. Of such mind were certain Goths, of whom it is written that, having in the spoil of a famous city taken a fair library, one hangman (belike fit to execute the fruits of their wits) who had murdered a great number of bodies, would have set fire in it: no, said another very gravely, take heed what you do, for while they are busy about these toys, we shall with more leisure conquer their countries. This indeed is the ordinary doctrine of ignorance, and many words sometimes I have heard spent in it. But because this reason is generally against all learning as well as poetry, or rather, all learning but poetry; because it were too large a digression to handle it, or at least too superfluous (since it is manifest that all government of action is to be gotten by knowledge, and knowledge best by gathering many knowledges, which is reading), I only, with Horace, to him that is of that opinion

jubeo stultum esse libenter;

for as for poetry itself, it is the freest from this objection.

For poetry is the companion of camps. I dare undertake, Orlando Furioso, or honest King Arthur, will never displease a soldier; but the quiddity of *ens* and *prima materia* will hardly agree with a corslet; and therefore, as I said in the beginning, even Turks and Tartars are delighted with poets. Homer, a Greek, flourished before Greece flourished. And if to a slight conjecture a conjecture may be opposed, truly it may seem, that as by him their learned men took almost their first light of knowledge, so their active men received their first motions of courage. Only

Alexander's example may serve, who by Plutarch is accounted of such virtue, that Fortune was not his guide but his footstool; whose acts speak for him, though Plutarch did not: indeed the phoenix of warlike princes. This Alexander left his schoolmaster, living Aristotle, behind 5 him, but took dead Homer with him. He put the philosopher Callisthenes to death for his seeming philosophical, indeed mutinous, stubbornness, but the chief thing he was ever heard to wish for was that Homer had been alive. He well found he received more bravery of mind by the 10 pattern of Achilles than by hearing the definition of fortitude. And therefore, if Cato misliked Fulvius for carrying Ennius with him to the field, it may be answered that, if Cato misliked it, the noble Fulvius liked it, or else he had not done it; for it was not the excellent Cato Uticensis 15 (whose authority I would much more have reverenced), but it was the former, in truth a bitter punisher of faults (but else a man that had never well sacrificed to the Graces: he misliked and cried out against all Greek learning, and yet, being eighty years old, began to learn it, belike fearing that 20 Pluto understood not Latin). Indeed, the Roman laws allowed no person to be carried to the wars but he that was in the soldiers' roll; and therefore, though Cato misliked his unmustered person, he misliked not his work. And if he had, Scipio Nasica, judged by common consent 25 the best Roman, loved him. Both the other Scipio brothers, who had by their virtues no less surnames than of Asia and Afric, so loved him that they caused his body to be buried in their sepulture. So as Cato's authority, being but against his person, and that answered with so far greater than 30 himself, is herein of no validity.

But now indeed my burden is great; now Plato's name [iv. Plato banished is laid upon me, whom, I must confess, of all philosophers I poets]

have ever esteemed most worthy of reverence, and with
good reason: since of all philosophers he is the most
poetical. Yet if he will defile the fountain out of which his
flowing streams have proceeded, let us boldly examine
5 with what reasons he did it. First, truly, a man might
maliciously object that Plato, being a philosopher, was a
natural enemy of poets. For indeed, after the philosophers
had picked out of the sweet mysteries of poetry the right
discerning true points of knowledge, they forthwith
10 putting it in method, and making a school-art of that which
the poets did only teach by a divine delightfulness, beginning to spurn at their guides, like ungrateful prentices,
were not content to set up shops for themselves, but sought
by all means to discredit their masters; which by the force
15 of delight being barred them, the less they could overthrow them, the more they hated them. For indeed, they
found for Homer seven cities strave who should have him
for their citizen; where many cities banished philosophers
as not fit members to live among them. For only repeating
20 certain of Euripides' verses, many Athenians had their
lives saved of the Syracusans, where the Athenians themselves thought many philosophers unworthy to live.
Certain poets, as Simonides and Pindar, had so prevailed
with Hiero the First, that of a tyrant they made him a just
25 king; where Plato could do so little with Dionysius, that he
himself of a philosopher was made a slave. But who should
do thus, I confess, should requite the objections made
against poets with like cavillations against philosophers;
as likewise one should do that should bid one read *Phaedrus*
30 or *Symposium* in Plato, or the discourse of love in Plutarch,
and see whether any poet do authorize abominable filthiness, as they do. Again, a man might ask out of what
commonwealth Plato did banish them: in sooth, thence

where he himself alloweth community of women—so
as belike this banishment grew not for effeminate wanton-
ness, since little should poetical sonnets be hurtful when a
man might have what woman he listed. But I honour
philosophical instructions, and bless the wits which bred 5
them: so as they be not abused, which is likewise stretched
to poetry.

Acts: 17   St. Paul himself (who yet, for the credit of poets,
To Titus: 1   twice citeth poets, and one of them by the
name of 'their prophet') setteth a watchword upon 10
philosophy—indeed upon the abuse. So doth Plato upon
the abuse, not upon poetry. Plato found fault that the poets
of his time filled the world with wrong opinions of the
gods, making light tales of that unspotted essence, and
therefore would not have the youth depraved with such 15
opinions. Herein may much be said. Let this suffice: the
poets did not induce such opinions, but did imitate those
opinions already induced. For all the Greek stories can well
testify that the very religion of that time stood upon many
and many-fashioned gods, not taught so by the poets, but 20
followed according to their nature of imitation. Who list
may read in Plutarch the discourses of Isis and Osiris, of
the cause why oracles ceased, of the divine providence, and
see whether the theology of that nation stood not upon
such dreams which the poets indeed superstitiously 25
observed—and truly (since they had not the light of Christ)
did much better in it than the philosophers, who, shaking
off superstition, brought in atheism. Plato therefore (whose
authority I had much rather justly construe than unjustly
resist) meant not in general of poets, in those words of 30
which Julius Scaliger saith *Qua authoritate barbari quidam
atque hispidi abuti velint ad poetas e republica exigendos;* but
only meant to drive out those wrong opinions of the Deity

(whereof now, without further law, Christianity hath taken away all the hurtful belief) perchance (as he thought) nourished by the then esteemed poets. And a man need go no further than to Plato himself to know his meaning:
5 who, in his dialogue called *Ion*, giveth high and rightly divine commendation unto poetry. So as Plato, banishing the abuse, not the thing, not banishing it, but giving due honour unto it, shall be our patron, and not our adversary. For indeed I had much rather (since truly I may do it)
10 show their mistaking of Plato (under whose lion's skin they would make an ass-like braying against poesy) than go about to overthrow his authority; whom, the wiser a man is, the more just cause he shall find to have in admiration; especially since he attributeth unto poesy more than
15 myself do, namely, to be a very inspiring of a divine force, far above man's wit, as in the forenamed dialogue is apparent.

   Of the other side, who would show the honours have been by the best sort of judgements granted them, a whole
20 sea of examples would present themselves: Alexanders, Caesars, Scipios, all favourers of poets; Laelius, called the Roman Socrates, himself a poet, so as part of *Heauton-timorumenos* in Terence was supposed to be made by him; and even the Greek Socrates, whom Apollo confirmed to
25 be the only wise man, is said to have spent part of his old time in putting Aesop's fables into verses. And therefore, full evil should it become his scholar Plato to put such words in his master's mouth against poets. But what need more? Aristotle writes the Art of Poesy; and why, if it
30 should not be written? Plutarch teacheth the use to be gathered of them; and how, if they should not be read? And who reads Plutarch's either history or philosophy, shall find he trimmeth both their garments with guards of

poesy. But I list not to defend poesy with the help of his underling historiography. Let it suffice to have showed it is a fit soil for praise to dwell upon; and what dispraise may be set upon it, is either easily overcome, or transformed into just commendation.   5

So that, since the excellencies of it may be so easily and so justly confirmed, and the low-creeping objections so soon trodden down: it not being an art of lies, but of true doctrine; not of effeminateness, but of notable stirring of courage; not of abusing man's wit, but of strengthening   10 man's wit; not banished, but honoured by Plato: let us rather plant more laurels for to engarland the poets' heads (which honour of being laureate, whereas besides them only triumphant captains were, is a sufficient authority to show the price they ought to be held in) than suffer the   15 ill-favoured breath of such wrong-speakers once to blow upon the clear springs of poesy.   [SUMMARY OF REFUTATION]

But since I have run so long a career in this matter, methinks, before I give my pen a full stop, it shall be but a little more lost time to inquire why England, the mother of   20 excellent minds, should be grown so hard a stepmother to poets, who certainly in wit ought to pass all other, since all only proceedeth from their wit, being indeed makers of themselves, not takers of others. How can I but exclaim   [DIGRESSION: ENGLAND]

Musa, mihi causas memora, quo numine laeso?   25

Sweet poesy, that hath anciently had kings, emperors, senators, great captains, such as, besides a thousand others, David, Adrian, Sophocles, Germanicus, not only to favour poets, but to be poets; and of our nearer times can present for her patrons a Robert, king of Sicily, the great King   30

Francis of France, King James of Scotland; such cardinals as
Bembus and Bibbiena; such famous preachers and teachers
as Beza and Melanchthon; so learned philosophers as
Fracastorius and Scaliger; so great orators as Pontanus and
Muretus; so piercing wits as George Buchanan; so grave
counsellors as, beside many, but before all, that Hospital
of France, than whom (I think) that realm never brought
forth a more accomplished judgement, more firmly
builded upon virtue: I say these, with numbers of others,
not only to read others' poesies, but to poetize for others'
reading—that poesy, thus embraced in all other places,
should only find in our time a hard welcome in England,
I think the very earth lamenteth it, and therefore decketh
our soil with fewer laurels than it was accustomed. For
heretofore poets have in England also flourished, and,
which is to be noted, even in those times when the trumpet
of Mars did sound loudest. And now that an overfaint
quietness should seem to strew the house for poets, they are
almost in as good reputation as the mountebanks at Venice.
Truly even that, as of the one side it giveth great praise to
poesy, which like Venus (but to better purpose) had
rather be troubled in the net with Mars than enjoy the
homely quiet of Vulcan: so serves it for a piece of a reason
why they are less grateful to idle England, which now can
scarce endure the pain of a pen.

Upon this necessarily followeth, that base men with
servile wits undertake it, who think it enough if they can
be rewarded of the printer. And so as Epaminondas is said
with the honour of his virtue to have made an office, by
his exercising it, which before was contemptible, to become
highly respected; so these men, no more but setting their
names to it, by their own disgracefulness disgrace the
most graceful poesy. For now, as if all the Muses were got

with child to bring forth bastard poets, without any
commission they do post over the banks of Helicon, till
they make the readers more weary than post-horses; while,
in the meantime, they

> Queis meliore luto finxit praecordia Titan   5

whose hearts the Titan has made of better clay

are better content to suppress the outflowings of their wit,
than, by publishing them, to be accounted knights of the
same order. But I that, before ever I durst aspire unto the
dignity, am admitted into the company of the paper-
blurrers, do find the very true cause of our wanting   10
estimation is want of desert—taking upon us to be poets
in despite of Pallas.

Now, wherein we want desert were a thankworthy
labour to express; but if I knew, I should have mended
myself. But I, as I never desired the title, so have I neglected   15
the means to come by it. Only, overmastered by some
thoughts, I yielded an inky tribute unto them. Marry, they
that delight in poesy itself should seek to know what they
do, and how they do; and especially look themselves in an
unflattering glass of reason, if they be inclinable unto it.   20
For poesy must not be drawn by the ears; it must be gently
led, or rather it must lead—which was partly the cause
that made the ancient-learned affirm it was a divine gift,
and no human skill: since all other knowledges lie ready
for any that hath strength of wit. A poet no industry can   25
make, if his own genius be not carried into it; and therefore it is an old proverb, *orator fit, poeta nascitur*.

Yet confess I always that as the fertilest ground must be
manured, so must the highest-flying wit have a Daedalus
to guide him. That Daedalus, they say, both in this and in   30
other, hath three wings to bear itself up into the air of due
commendation: that is, art, imitation, and exercise. But

art, imitation, exercise

these, neither artificial rules nor imitative patterns, we much cumber ourselves withal. Exercise indeed we do, but that very fore-backwardly: for where we should exercise to know, we exercise as having known; and so is our brain
5 delivered of much matter which never was begotten by knowledge. For there being two principal parts, matter to be expressed by words and words to express the matter, in neither we use art or imitation rightly. Our matter is *quodlibet* indeed, though wrongly performing Ovid's
10 verse,

Quicquid conabor dicere, versus erit;

never marshalling it into any assured rank, that almost the readers cannot tell where to find themselves.

[I. MATTER poetry] Chaucer, undoubtedly, did excellently in his *Troilus and Criseyde;* of whom, truly, I know not whether to marvel more, either that he in that misty time could see so clearly, or that we in this clear age go so stumblingly after him. Yet had he great wants, fit to be forgiven in so reverent an antiquity. I account the *Mirror of Magistrates* meetly
20 furnished of beautiful parts, and in the Earl of Surrey's lyrics many things tasting of a noble birth, and worthy of a noble mind. The *Shepherds' Calendar* hath much poetry in his eclogues, indeed worthy the reading, if I be not deceived. (That same framing of his style to an old rustic
25 language I dare not allow, since neither Theocritus in Greek, Virgil in Latin, nor Sannazzaro in Italian did affect it.) Besides these I do not remember to have seen but few (to speak boldly) printed that have poetical sinews in them; for proof whereof, let but most of the verses be put
30 in prose, and then ask the meaning, and it will be found that one verse did but beget another, without ordering at the first what should be at the last; which becomes a

confused mass of words, with a tingling sound of rhyme, barely accompanied with reason.

Our tragedies and comedies (not without cause cried [drama] out against), observing rules neither of honest civility nor skilful poetry—excepting *Gorboduc* (again, I say, of those 5 that I have seen), which notwithstanding as it is full of stately speeches and well-sounding phrases, climbing to the height of Seneca's style, and as full of notable morality, which it doth most delightfully teach, and so obtain the very end of poesy, yet in truth it is very defectuous in 10 the circumstances, which grieveth me, because it might not remain as an exact model of all tragedies. For it is faulty both in place and time, the two necessary companions of all corporal actions. For where the stage should always represent but one place, and the uttermost time presupposed 15 in it should be, both by Aristotle's precept and common reason, but one day, there is both many days, and many places, inartificially imagined.

But if it be so in *Gorboduc*, how much more in all the [unity of place] rest, where you shall have Asia of the one side, and Afric 20 of the other, and so many other under-kingdoms, that the player, when he cometh in, must ever begin with telling where he is, or else the tale will not be conceived? Now you shall have three ladies walk to gather flowers: and then we must believe the stage to be a garden. By and by 25 we hear news of shipwreck in the same place: and then we are to blame if we accept it not for a rock. Upon the back of that comes out a hideous monster with fire and smoke: and then the miserable beholders are bound to take it for a cave. While in the meantime two armies fly in, represented 30 with four swords and bucklers: and then what hard heart will not receive it for a pitched field?

Now, of time they are much more liberal: for ordinary [unity of time]

c

it is that two young princes fall in love; after many traverses, she is got with child, delivered of a fair boy; he is lost, groweth a man, falls in love, and is ready to get another child; and all this in two hours' space: which, 5 how absurd it is in sense, even sense may imagine, and art hath taught, and all ancient examples justified—and at this day, the ordinary players in Italy will not err in. Yet will some bring in an example of *Eunuchus* in Terence, that containeth matter of two days, yet far short of twenty 10 years. True it is, and so was it to be played in two days, and so fitted to the time it set forth. And though Plautus have in one place done amiss, let us hit with him, and not miss with him.

[the three unities] But they will say: How then shall we set forth a story 15 which containeth both many places and many times? And do they not know that a tragedy is tied to the laws of poesy, and not of history; not bound to follow the story, but having liberty either to feign a quite new matter or to frame the history to the most tragical conveniency? 20 Again, many things may be told which cannot be showed, if they know the difference betwixt reporting and representing. As, for example, I may speak (though I am here) of Peru, and in speech digress from that to the description of Calicut; but in action I cannot represent it without 25 Pacolet's horse; and so was the manner the ancients took, by some *Nuntius* to recount things done in former time or other place. Lastly, if they will represent a history, they must not (as Horace saith) begin *ab ovo*, but they must come to the principal point of that one action which they 30 will represent.

By example this will be best expressed. I have a story of young Polydorus, delivered for safety's sake, with great riches, by his father Priam to Polymnestor, king of Thrace, in the Trojan war time; he, after some years, hearing the overthrow of Priam, for to make the treasure his own, murdereth the child; the body of the child is taken up by Hecuba; she, the same day, findeth a sleight to be revenged most cruelly of the tyrant. Where now would one of our tragedy writers begin, but with the delivery of the child? Then should he sail over into Thrace, and so spend I know not how many years, and travel numbers of places. But where doth Euripides? Even with the finding of the body, leaving the rest to be told by the spirit of Polydorus. This need no further to be enlarged; the dullest wit may conceive it.

But besides these gross absurdities, how all their plays be neither right tragedies, nor right comedies, mingling kings and clowns, not because the matter so carrieth it, but thrust in the clown by head and shoulders to play a part in majestical matters with neither decency nor discretion, so as neither the admiration and commiseration, nor the right sportfulness, is by their mongrel tragi-comedy obtained. I know Apuleius did somewhat so, but that is a thing recounted with space of time, not represented in one moment; and I know the ancients have one or two examples of tragi-comedies, as Plautus hath *Amphitryo*; but, if we mark them well, we shall find that they never, or very daintily, match hornpipes and funerals. So falleth it out that, having indeed no right comedy, in that comical part of our tragedy, we have nothing but scurrility, unworthy of any chaste ears, or some extreme show of doltishness, indeed fit to lift up a loud laughter, and nothing else: where the whole tract of a comedy should be full of delight, as the tragedy should be still maintained in a well-raised admiration.

But our comedians think there is no delight without

[decorum]

[delight and laughter]

laughter; which is very wrong, for though laughter may
come with delight, yet cometh it not of delight, as though
delight should be the cause of laughter; but well may one
thing breed both together. Nay, rather in themselves they
5 have, as it were, a kind of contrariety: for delight we
scarcely do but in things that have a conveniency to ourselves or to the general nature; laughter almost ever
cometh of things most disproportioned to ourselves and
nature. Delight hath a joy in it, either permanent or present.
10 Laughter hath only a scornful tickling.

For example, we are ravished with delight to see a fair
woman, and yet are far from being moved to laughter; we
laugh at deformed creatures, wherein certainly we cannot
delight. We delight in good chances, we laugh at mis-
15 chances: we delight to hear the happiness of our friends,
or country, at which he were worthy to be laughed at
that would laugh; we shall, contrarily, laugh sometimes to
find a matter quite mistaken and go down the hill against
the bias in the mouth of some such men—as for the respect
20 of them one shall be heartily sorry, he cannot choose but
laugh, and so is rather pained than delighted with laughter.

Yet deny I not but that they may go well together. For
as in Alexander's picture well set out we delight without
laughter, and in twenty mad antics we laugh without
25 delight; so in Hercules, painted with his great beard and
furious countenance, in a woman's attire, spinning at
Omphale's commandment, it breedeth both delight and
laughter: for the representing of so strange a power in love
procureth delight, and the scornfulness of the action stirreth
30 laughter. But I speak to this purpose, that all the end of the
comical part be not upon such scornful matters as stir
laughter only, but, mixed with it, that delightful teaching
which is the end of poesy. And the great fault even in that

difference
between
delight &
laughter

point of laughter, and forbidden plainly by Aristotle, is
that they stir laughter in sinful things, which are rather
execrable than ridiculous, or in miserable, which are rather
to be pitied than scorned. For what is it to make folks gape
at a wretched beggar and a beggarly clown; or, against 5
law of hospitality, to jest at strangers, because they speak
not English so well as we do? What do we learn, since it
is certain

> Nil habet infelix paupertas durius in se,
> Quam quod ridiculos homines facit?   10

But rather, a busy loving courtier and a heartless threaten-
ing Thraso; a self-wise-seeming schoolmaster; an awry-
transformed traveller. These if we saw walk in stage names,
which we play naturally, therein were delightful laughter,
and teaching delightfulness—as in the other, the tragedies 15
of Buchanan do justly bring forth a divine admiration.

But I have lavished out too many words of this play
matter. I do it because, as they are excelling parts of poesy,
so is there none so much used in England, and none can
be more pitifully abused; which, like an unmannerly 20
daughter showing a bad education, causeth her mother
Poesy's honesty to be called in question.

Other sort of poetry almost have we none, but that lyrical [love poetry]
kind of songs and sonnets: which, Lord, if He gave us
so good minds, how well it might be employed, and with 25
how heavenly fruit, both private and public, in singing the
praises of the immortal beauty: the immortal goodness
of that God who giveth us hands to write and wits to
conceive; of which we might well want words, but never
matter; of which we could turn our eyes to nothing, but 30
we should ever have new-budding occasions. But truly
many of such writings as come under the banner of unresist-
ible love, if I were a mistress, would never persuade me

they were in love: so coldly they apply fiery speeches, as
men that had rather read lovers' writings—and so caught
up certain swelling phrases which hang together like a man
that once told my father that the wind was at north-west
5 and by south, because he would be sure to name winds
enough—than that in truth they feel those passions, which
easily (as I think) may be bewrayed by that same forcible-
ness or *energia* (as the Greeks call it) of the writer. But let
this be a sufficient though short note, that we miss the
10 right use of the material point of poesy.

[2. DICTION]   Now, for the outside of it, which is words, or (as I may
term it) diction, it is even well worse. So is that honey-
flowing matron Eloquence apparelled, or rather disguised,
in a courtesan-like painted affectation: one time, with so
15 far-fet words that may seem monsters but must seem
strangers to any poor Englishman; another time, with
coursing of a letter, as if they were bound to follow the
method of a dictionary; another time, with figures and
flowers, extremely winter-starved. But I would this fault
20 were only peculiar to versifiers, and had not as large
possession among prose-printers; and (which is to be
marvelled) among many scholars; and (which is to be
pitied) among some preachers. Truly I could wish, if at
least I might be so bold to wish in a thing beyond the
25 reach of my capacity, the diligent imitators of Tully and
Demosthenes (most worthy to be imitated) did not so much
keep Nizolian paper-books of their figures and phrases,
as by attentive translation (as it were) devour them whole,
and make them wholly theirs: for now they cast sugar and
30 spice upon every dish that is served to the table—like those
Indians, not content to wear earrings at the fit and natural
place of the ears, but they will thrust jewels through their
nose and lips, because they will be sure to be fine. Tully,

when he was to drive out Catiline, as it were with a
thunderbolt of eloquence, often used the figure of
repetition, as *Vivit. Vivit? Imo in senatum venit*, &c. Indeed,
inflamed with a well-grounded rage, he would have his
words (as it were) double out of his mouth, and so do that 5
artificially which we see men in choler do naturally. And
we, having noted the grace of those words, hale them in
sometimes to a familiar epistle, when it were too too much
choler to be choleric. How well store of *similiter cadences*
doth sound with the gravity of the pulpit, I would but 10
invoke Demosthenes' soul to tell, who with a rare daintiness
useth them. Truly they have made me think of the sophister that with too much subtlety would prove two eggs
three, and though he might be counted a sophister, had
none for his labour. So these men bringing in such a kind 15
of eloquence, well may they obtain an opinion of a seeming
finesse, but persuade few—which should be the end of
their finesse. Now for similitudes, in certain printed discourses, I think all herbarists, all stories of beasts, fowls, and
fishes are rifled up, that they come in multitudes to wait 20
upon any of our conceits; which certainly is as absurd a
surfeit to the ears as is possible. For the force of a similitude
not being to prove anything to a contrary disputer, but
only to explain to a willing hearer, when that is done, the
rest is a most tedious prattling, rather over-swaying the 25
memory from the purpose whereto they were applied,
than any whit informing the judgement, already either
satisfied, or by similitudes not to be satisfied. For my part,
I do not doubt, when Antonius and Crassus, the great
forefathers of Cicero in eloquence, the one (as Cicero 30
testifieth of them) pretended not to know art, the other
not to set by it, because with a plain sensibleness they might
win credit of popular ears (which credit is the nearest step

[margin annotation: simile: to explain not to prove (for memory rather than judgment) See note p105]

to persuasion, which persuasion is the chief mark of
oratory), I do not doubt (I say) but that they used these
knacks very sparingly; which who doth generally use, any
man may see doth dance to his own music, and so be noted
5 by the audience more careful to speak curiously than to
speak truly. Undoubtedly (at least to my opinion undoubtedly), I have found in divers smally learned courtiers
a more sound style than in some professors of learning; of
which I can guess no other cause, but that the courtier,
10 following that which by practice he findeth fittest to
nature, therein (though he know it not) doth according to
art, though not by art: where the other, using art to show
art, and not to hide art (as in these cases he should do),
flieth from nature, and indeed abuseth art.

[English language]   But what? Methinks I deserve to be pounded for straying
from poetry to oratory. But both have such an affinity in
the wordish consideration, that I think this digression will
make my meaning receive the fuller understanding: which
is not to take upon me to teach poets how they should do,
20 but only, finding myself sick among the rest, to show
some one or two spots of the common infection grown
among the most part of writers, that, acknowledging
ourselves somewhat awry, we may bend to the right use
both of matter and manner: whereto our language giveth
25 us great occasion, being indeed capable of any excellent
exercising of it. I know some will say it is a mingled
language. And why not so much the better, taking the
best of both the other? Another will say it wanteth grammar. Nay truly, it hath that praise, that it wants not
30 grammar: for grammar it might have, but it needs it not,
being so easy in itself, and so void of those cumbersome
differences of cases, genders, moods, and tenses, which I
think was a piece of the Tower of Babylon's curse, that a

cf Castiglione
Bk I

man should be put to school to learn his mother-tongue. But for the uttering sweetly and properly the conceits of the mind (which is the end of speech), that hath it equally with any other tongue in the world; and is particularly happy in compositions of two or three words together, near the Greek, far beyond the Latin, which is one of the greatest beauties can be in a language.

Now of versifying there are two sorts, the one ancient, [English verse] the other modern: the ancient marked the quantity of each syllable, and according to that framed his verse; the modern, observing only number (with some regard of the accent), the chief life of it standeth in that like sounding of the words, which we call rhyme. Whether of these be the more excellent, would bear many speeches: the ancient (no doubt) more fit for music, both words and time observing quantity, and more fit lively to express diverse passions, by the low or lofty sound of the well-weighed syllable; the latter likewise, with his rhyme, striketh a certain music to the ear, and, in fine, since it doth delight, though by another way, it obtains the same purpose: there being in either sweetness, and wanting in neither majesty. Truly the English, before any vulgar language I know, is fit for both sorts. For, for the ancient, the Italian is so full of vowels that it must ever be cumbered with elisions; the Dutch so, of the other side, with consonants, that they cannot yield the sweet sliding, fit for a verse; the French in his whole language hath not one word that hath his accent in the last syllable saving two, called *antepenultima*; and little more hath the Spanish, and therefore very gracelessly may they use dactyls. The English is subject to none of these defects. Now for the rhyme, though we do not observe quantity, yet we observe the accent very precisely, which other languages either cannot do, or will not do so

absolutely. That *caesura,* or breathing place in the midst of the verse, neither Italian nor Spanish have, the French and we never almost fail of. Lastly, even the very rhyme itself, the Italian cannot put it in the last syllable, by the French
5 named the masculine rhyme, but still in the next to the last, which the French call the female, or the next before that, which the Italian term *sdrucciola.* The example of the former is *buono: suono,* of the *sdrucciola* is *femina: semina.* The French, of the other side, hath both the male, as
10 *bon: son,* and the female, as *plaise: taise,* but the *sdrucciola* he hath not: where the English hath all three, as *due: true, father: rather, motion: potion*—with much more which might be said, but that already I find the triflingness of this discourse is much too much enlarged.

[PERORATION] So that since the ever-praiseworthy Poesy is full of virtue-breeding delightfulness, and void of no gift that ought to be in the noble name of learning; since the blames laid against it are either false or feeble; since the cause why it is not esteemed in England is the fault of poet-apes, not poets;
20 since, lastly, our tongue is most fit to honour poesy, and to be honoured by poesy; I conjure you all that have had the evil luck to read this ink-wasting toy of mine, even in the name of the nine Muses, no more to scorn the sacred mysteries of poesy; no more to laugh at the name of poets,
25 as though they were next inheritors to fools; no more to jest at the reverent title of a rhymer; but to believe, with Aristotle, that they were the ancient treasurers of the Grecians' divinity; to believe, with Bembus, that they were first bringers-in of all civility; to believe, with Scaliger,
30 that no philosopher's precepts can sooner make you an honest man than the reading of Virgil; to believe, with Clauserus, the translator of Cornutus, that it pleased the

heavenly Deity, by Hesiod and Homer, under the veil of fables, to give us all knowledge, logic, rhetoric, philosophy natural and moral, and *quid non?*; to believe, with me, that there are many mysteries contained in poetry, which of purpose were written darkly, lest by profane wits it should 5 be abused; to believe, with Landino, that they are so beloved of the gods that whatsoever they write proceeds of a divine fury; lastly, to believe themselves, when they tell you they will make you immortal by their verses. Thus doing, your name shall flourish in the printers' shops; 10 thus doing, you shall be of kin to many a poetical preface; thus doing, you shall be most fair, most rich, most wise, most all, you shall dwell upon superlatives; thus doing, though you be *libertino patre natus*, you shall suddenly grow *Herculea proles*,   15

Si quid mea carmina possunt;

thus doing, your soul shall be placed with Dante's Beatrice, or Virgil's Anchises. But if (fie of such a but) you be born so near the dull-making cataract of Nilus that you cannot hear the planet-like music of poetry; if you have so earth- 20 creeping a mind that it cannot lift itself up to look to the sky of poetry, or rather, by a certain rustical disdain, will become such a mome as to be a Momus of poetry; then, though I will not wish unto you the ass's ears of Midas, nor to be driven by a poet's verses, as Bubonax was, to hang 25 himself, nor to be rhymed to death, as is said to be done in Ireland; yet thus much curse I must send you, in the behalf of all poets, that while you live, you live in love, and never get favour for lacking skill of a sonnet; and, when you die, your memory die from the earth for want of an epitaph. 30

NOTES

p. 17, l. 1. *the right virtuous Edward Wotton* (1548–1626), courtier and diplomatist, with whom Sidney became close friends at the Court of the Emperor Maximilian II in Vienna in 1574/5 and returned to England in June 1575. 'Right virtuous', a 'titular' rendering of the common humanist epithet *prudentissimus* and applied to Sidney himself on Olney's title-page, already points to the central theme of the *Defence*.

p. 17, l. 3. *horsemanship*, both the practice and the 'contemplations' (theory), in which Sidney was much interested. Chivalresque jousts and tournaments were a special feature of the Elizabethan court-festivals.

p. 17, l. 4. *esquire*, equerry, officer in charge of the royal stables.

p. 17, l. 12. *faculty*, department of learning.

p. 17, l. 15. *abiders*, stayers.

p. 17, l. 19. *pedanteria*, mere book-learning. Sidney 'quotes' Pugliano by using the Italian word.

p. 17, l. 23. *a piece of*, a bit of.

p. 17, ll. 24–25. *wished myself a horse*. Eulogies of beasts and other unlikely subjects were frequently used as rhetorical exercises (cf. 49.22 ff. n.). 'Ass' (or 'horse') and 'man' were, moreover, common syllogistic terms.

p. 18, l. 7. *master*, ironic reference to Pugliano.

p. 18, l. 11. *available*, valid.

the former, *viz.* horsemanship.

p. 18, l. 22. *the hedgehog*, an allusion to the pseudo-Aesopic fable of the snake and the hedgehog.

p. 18, l. 23. *the vipers*, an allusion to Pliny, *Natural History*, x.lxxxii, a favourite Elizabethan image of ingratitude.

p. 18, l. 26. *Musaeus*, a legendary pre-Homeric figure, associated with certain religious poems.

p. 18, l. 27. *Hesiod* (*fl.* eighth century B.C.), author of *Theogony* and *Works and Days*.

p. 18, l. 29. *Orpheus*, son of a Muse and revealer of religious mysteries, long associated with the 'Orphic hymns', was a central figure in Renaissance thought, representing harmony revealed through religious poetry and music.

Linus, a legendary poet, Orpheus' teacher.

p. 18, l. 32. *challenge*, claim.

p. 19, l. 5. *Amphion*, mythological figure whose power as a poet and musician was frequently compared with that of Orpheus.

p. 19, l. 7. *indeed stony and beastly people*. Sidney agrees with other commentators who read these anecdotes as meaning, elliptically, that Amphion's harp and Orpheus' lute could move hard-hearted, savage people—for instance, move them to build Thebes.

p. 19, l. 8. *Livius Andronicus* (d. 204 B.C.), a Greek, the first Latin poet.

Ennius (239–169 B.C.), teacher and author of a verse history of Rome, the epic *Annals*.

p. 19, l. 10. *science*, Lat. *scientia*, knowledge.

p. 19, ll. 10–11. *Dante, Boccaccio, and Petrarch . . . Gower and Chaucer*. These five poets are listed because, to Sidney, each of them was 'the first' in some particular field of poetry and at the same time a 'scientist'—i.e. a scholar-philosopher.

p. 19, l. 13. *fore-going*, lead.

p. 19, l. 17. *Thales* of Miletus (*fl. c.* 600 B.C.), the first of the Seven Wise Men of Greece, is supposed to have composed scientific works in verse.

Empedocles (*fl.* 450 B.C.), the Sicilian scientist-poet, who by some was said to have met his death by jumping into the crater of Mount Etna, thinking he was a god (cf. Horace, *Art of Poetry* 465).

Parmenides of Elea (*fl. c.* 500 B.C.), author of a poem *On Nature*. Note that Sidney here applies the formal criterion verse=poetry, which he later abandons (27.15 ff.; 50.9 ff.).

p. 19, l. 18. *Pythagoras* of Samos (*fl.* 530 B.C.), supposed author of the *Golden Sayings*.

p. 19, l. 19. *Phocylides* of Miletus (*fl.* 560 B.C.), a gnomic poet.

Tyrtaeus (*fl.* 670 B.C.), the lame Athenian schoolmaster whose poems inspired the Spartans to victory.

p. 19, l. 20. *Solon* (*fl.* 600 B.C.), Athenian legislator, one of the Seven Wise Men. In *Critias* Plato gives an account of the vanished continent of Atlantis, the subject of a (now lost) epic by Solon.

p. 19, l. 26. *even Plato.* Not only did sixteenth-century humanists consider Plato's 'feigned narratives' poetic—the element of fiction introduces a more properly Sidneian notion of 'poetry' (cf. 19.17 n.)—but the Platonic dialogue, banquet, and garden or country walk became commonplace settings in their literary compositions.

p. 20, l. 2. *Gyges' ring*, the ring found by Gyges, a shepherd, in the Underworld, which enabled him to become invisible and be made King of Lydia (*Republic* II. 359).

p. 20, l. 8. *Herodotus* of Halicarnassus (484–c. 425 B.C.), whose *History* was later divided into nine books, each named after one of the nine Muses.

p. 20, l. 21. *Turkey.* In Sidney's time the Turks, who had penetrated into central Europe as far as Hungary, were a common threat to the (otherwise much divided) Christian world. In his correspondence with Hubert Languet they are frequently discussed (cf. 46.16 n.)

law–giving divines, muftis.

p. 20, l. 23. *Ireland*, the unruliest part of Queen Elizabeth's realm, with which the Sidneys were personally associated. His father, Sir Henry Sidney, had long been its Lord Deputy (rendered in Latin as *Prorex*, which detail was invariably stressed when Philip Sidney travelled abroad: it suggested diplomatically that in matters of protocol the son of a *Rex*—although this son was in fact titleless—is by implication a kind of prince). Sidney shared an interest in Ireland with many of his acquaintances, e.g. Edmund Spenser.

p. 20, l. 27. *areytos.* The exploration of the rich Americas, in which Sidney had actually invested some money, was one of the most fascinating pursuits of his age. He himself, however, had never seen the New World, and his knowledge of the *areyto*, a ceremonial dance accompanied by songs praising the deeds of ancestors, probably derives from Peter Martyr's *Decades*, III.vii (Eng. trsl. 1555).

p. 20, l. 33. *Wales.* In this period various antiquaries were actively studying ancient survivals in Wales, and attempted to trace the earliest, and largely mythological, history of Britain (cf. 56.2).

Sidney, who had certain associations with these regions—e.g. through his sister Mary, married to the Earl of Pembroke in 1577—was much interested in their researches.

p. 21, l. 23. *Albinus*, Governor of Britain in A.D. 192, acclaimed Emperor by his soldiers in the following year, took up arms against Septimius Severus, and was defeated and killed near Lyon in A.D. 197.

p. 21, l. 25. *Arma amens* &c., 'Frantic I seize arms; yet little purpose is there in arms' (*Aeneid* II.314).

p. 21, l. 32. *Delphos*, Delphi, 'the navel of the earth', where, in the great temple of Apollo, the Pythia's oracles were delivered.

Sibylla, an ancient prophetess whose name was attached to a constantly increasing collection of prophetic writings.

p. 22, l. 3. *conceit*, mental conception, idea (cf. 28.10 ff. n; 24.17 n.).

p. 22, l. 7. *Psalms*. The Psalms, regarded as divine poems, in vernacular translations played a central part in the religious and literary movements of the sixteenth century. Sidney himself translated a number of them.

p. 22, l. 13. *merely*, entirely.

p. 22, l. 16. *prosopopeias*, from προσωποποιία, personification, a rhetorical figure by which an imaginary or absent person is represented as speaking or acting.

p. 22, l. 18. *poesy*, ποίησις, the art of making (poetry), which Sidney normally distinguishes from poetry, Lat. *poetria*, the general product of this art. The individual product is the poem (ποίημα, i.e. a thing made), cf. 22.29 ff.

almost, indeed.

p. 22, l. 24. *quiet judgements*. The gradual introduction of prescribed psalm-singing in public worship continued to meet with some Puritan opposition, and had before been criticized by right-wing Anglicans.

p. 22, l. 33. *have met with*, agree with.

p. 23, l. 1. *a maker*, a common Northern word for 'poet' in the sixteenth century. To 'make' is used in M.E. (and by Spenser) for to 'write verse', in Chaucer with special reference to writing in the vernacular.

p. 23, l. 6. *nature*, the created world. There are various similarities between the following pages and the opening paragraphs of Scaliger's authoritative work *Poetices Libri VII* (1561) from which Sidney may have borrowed some of his arguments.

p. 23, l. 15. *standeth upon*, is concerned with.

p. 23, l. 16. *follow nature*, the Stoic precept, repeated throughout the Renaissance and after, its meaning varying according to intention, and interpretation of the word 'nature'.

p. 23, l. 22. *are compassed within the circle of a question*, are limited by the scope and purpose of the questions they answer (cf. 26.14 n.). Here, as elsewhere, Sidney is doing the established *artes* less than justice, so that he may bring out the infinite scope of poetry the more clearly and startlingly.

p. 23, l. 25. *the metaphysic*, metaphysician, is concerned with how 'realities' exist in man's mind; but, Sidney adds, such 'abstract and second notions' derive from first notions ('reality') so that, basically, the metaphysician is also dependent upon 'nature'.

p. 23, l. 30. *another nature*. A poet's 'invention' may, in other words, create a world which little resembles 'reality' as we know it (cf. 24.32 n.; 25.2 ff. n.).

p. 24, l. 3. *zodiac*. The celestial zodiac being the circle within which nature is confined, the zodiac of man's wit (intellect) necessarily defines the limit of poetic 'nature'.

p. 24, l. 7. *brazen*, like the third age of Ovid's *Metamorphoses* I.125, preceded by the ages of silver and gold. The return to the first or Golden Age—a literary commonplace, especially in pastoral poetry—represented the return to the full knowledge of perfection: it was not a mere aesthetic pursuit of beauty.

p. 24, l. 8. *for whom* &c. The earth was created for the use of man, upon whom special gifts were bestowed (cf. Genesis i: 26 ff.; Psalm viii).

p. 24, l. 11. *Theagenes* of Thessaly, Chariclea's lover in the popular fourth-century romance *Aethiopica* by Heliodorus, Bishop of Tricca in Thessaly.

p. 24, l. 12. *Pylades*, the faithful friend of Orestes, as described in Greek tragedy.

D

Orlando, the hero of Ariosto's epic poem *Orlando Furioso*, and of various other heroic works.

p. 24, l. 13. *Cyrus* (d. 529 B.C.), founder of the great Persian state, whose noble qualities are recounted in Xenophon's *Cyropaedia*. He was constantly quoted as a model of manly virtue, and appears to have had a special fascination for Sidney (cf. 27.20; 33.27; 35.25; 36.1; 37.3; 40.21; 47.6; 54.2).

p. 24, l. 14. *Aeneas*, extolled by almost every humanist as the poetic perfection of manhood, Virgil's *Aeneid* being the universal example of poetic excellence in the great epic genre.

p. 24, l. 15. *the works of the one be essential*, the works of nature actually 'are'.

p. 24, l. 17. *that idea or fore-conceit*. According to Sidney's interpretation of a fundamentally Platonic argument, the essence of poetry is not 'in the work itself' but in the poet's ability to invent original (and valid) concepts or 'ideas'—ἰδέα, from ἰδεῖν, to see (cf. 28.10 ff. n.).

p. 24, l. 21. *not wholly imaginative*, not merely as images in the mind, and therefore without validity and substance.

p. 24, l. 23. *not only to make a Cyrus*. Cyrus is not a 'natural' specimen, but a 'poetic' example of perfection worthy to be studied and followed.

p. 24, l. 26. *that maker*, that poet, i.e. Xenophon, whose *Cyropaedia* was looked upon as a handbook for princes.

p. 24, l. 32. *second nature*. The nature over the works of which man is still master (cf. 24.8 n.) is not the undecaying (because perfect) nature as 'the heavenly Maker' first created it: it is a 'second nature', become imperfect since.

he, i.e. man.

p. 25, l. 1. *her*, i.e. nature's.

p. 25, l. 2. *the credulous of*, those disposed to believe in.

Adam &c. At the end of his exposition of fundamentals, Sidney adds a personal, religious overtone, although he realizes that his arguments may be shared by few. Sinful man cannot recover the perfections of the first state of nature because, since 'that first accursed fall of Adam', his will is no longer wholly bent upon truth and goodness. But his wit—i.e. the rational intellect which is characteristic of man and which relates man to his Maker—may still be 'erected' in an attempt to gain 'ideas' of lost perfections. Sidney's poet is a man who cultivates this ability to the utmost of his powers. His 'ideas', being ideas of 'first nature', 'with the force of a divine breath' show 'another nature', to an imperfect world that lives in 'second nature'. Thus poesy is the effort of an individual mind to bridge the gap between the sinful state and the lost paradise, or 'golden' world of man.

The last few lines not only provide a clue to the essence of Sidney's theory, but also explain the unique value Sidney attaches to the art of poetry.

p. 25, l. 9. *opening*, exposition.

p. 25, l. 15 ff. *Poesy therefore* &c. For his proposed definition of poesy Sidney makes no attempt at originality but borrows three commonplaces of sixteenth-century literary theory, based mainly upon, respectively, Aristotle, Plutarch, and Horace: 1. poesy is *mimesis* or imitation, i.e. a representation of images of something else—'ideas'; 2. in representing these images verbally, a poem is, as it were, a painting in words; 3. but art is only a means towards an end, and the aim of the art of poesy is 'to teach and delight'.

p. 25, l. 26. *Emanuel Tremellius* (1510–80), orientalist, and the French theologian *Franciscus Junius* (1545–1602), Protestant authors of a famous Latin Bible translation, published at Frankfurt a few years before the *Defence* was written. Scaliger gives only classical-pagan instances of theological poetry, Sidney characteristically substitutes Christian examples.

p. 25, l. 28. *the Holy Ghost*, who caused the poetic books to be written.

p. 25, l. 30. *Homer*, to whom certain rhapsodic pieces were often ascribed.

p. 26, l. 1. James v:13.

p. 26, l. 7. *Cato*, third-century author of a Latin ethical treatise, the *Distichs*, used for centuries as a school-textbook.

p. 26, l. 8. *Lucretius* (95–52 B.C.), author of a poem *On Nature*.

p. 26, l. 9. *Manilius*, Roman poet in the days of Augustus, author of *Astronomica*.

Pontanus, Giovanni Pontano (1426–1503), politician, scholar, and neo-Latin poet, author of *Urania*.

Lucan (A.D. 39–65), author of *Pharsalia*.

p. 26, l. 14. *the proposed subject*. Such poems are necessarily limited by the topics of the propositions they deal with, whereas true poetry may invent an infinite variety of topics (cf. 'the circle of a question' and 'the proposed matter', 23.22 n.). It had been argued, therefore, that 'this second sort' was verse, not poetry. Sidney, who evidently enjoyed their 'sweetly uttered knowledge', however limited in scope, leaves the dispute to others.

p. 26, ll. 17–18 ff. *betwixt whom* &c. The 'second sort' of poets (or painters) are necessarily minor artists, because they copy out particular things for their own sake, unlike the third category who invent new 'ideas'.

p. 26, l. 23. *Lucretia*, the Roman wife who, having been violated by Sextus Tarquinius, killed herself and so redeemed her lost honour was a favourite theme in Renaissance painting.

p. 26, l. 26. ff. *For these third* &c. These, the 'right poets', represent not what is, but what their judicious minds have learned to conceive of as probable or desirable (cf. 23.28 ff.).

p. 26, l. 31. *the first and most noble sort*, i.e. the theological and divine poets.

p. 26, l. 32. *these*, i.e. the third category, true 'makers'.

p. 27, l. 1. *do merely make to imitate*, write poetry only as an art of 'imitation'.

p. 27, l. 2. *delight*. Unlike some sixteenth-century theorists, Sidney looks upon delight as an essential ingredient in the whole process of rhetorical persuasion, but no more.

p. 27, l. 6. *scope*, mark for aiming at, purpose.

p. 27, ll. 10–11. *heroic* &c. The number of genres varied from critic to critic. Sidney's subdivision into eight 'denominations', which he evidently gave in order of importance (cf. 42.30 ff.), is remarkable only for the unusually high position of the lyrical genre.

p. 27, l. 15. *numbrous*, metrical.

p. 27, l. 17. *ornament and no cause*. Sidney stresses a somewhat unorthodox aspect of his theory, *viz.* that verse is not essential to poetry: his definition of poetry covers many prose-works—e.g. his own *Arcadia* (cf. 50.9 ff).

p. 27, l. 22. *as Cicero saith*, in *Epistles to Quintus* I.i.8.

p. 27, l. 24. *Heliodorus*, see 24.11 n.

sugared, sweet and subtle.

p. 27, l. 32. *note*, distinguishing characteristic.

p. 28, l. 1. *all in all*, all things in all respects.

p. 28, l. 4. *peising*, weighing. Verse should aim at verbal precision and propriety of diction.

p. 28, l. 9. *sentence*, i.e. not 'penalty' but 'judgement'.

p. 28, l. 10. ff. *This purifying of wit* &c. The process of perfecting man's wit (i.e. intellect or understanding), to which the art of dialectic (here substituted significantly by the art of poesy) is devoted, may be divided into three parts: a. *memory*, the ability to store arguments, b. *judgement*, the ability to arrange them, and c. *conceit*, the ability to invent new ones. 'Learning', i.e. the cultivation of these three parts of the understanding, 'purifies' man's wit, compensating for his 'infected will' (25.2 ff. n.). Cf. 71.21 ff. n.

cf pp 104-5

p. 28, l. 14. ff. *the final end* &c. The aim of all learning is to know perfection, or, in Platonic terms, to achieve a release from the prison of man's body to return to a full and natural understanding of the 'ideas' (cf. 24.17 n.). But Sidney makes one reservation: the 'first accursed fall of Adam' (cf. 25.2 ff. n.) which stands in the way of complete perfection.

p. 28, l. 17. *inclination*, natural disposition.

p. 28, l. 28. *his own divine essence*, see 25.2 ff. n., and cf. 28.14 n.

p. 28, l. 30. *a ditch*, cf. Sidney's *Astrophil and Stella* xix, which also gives Plato's popular story of the astronomer.

p. 28, l. 32. *a straight line*, a commonplace from Seneca's 88th epistle.

p. 29, l. 5. ἀρχιτεκτονική, architektonike, the art that pursues the greatest common good, to the furthering of which the others are devoted and to which they are therefore subordinated (cf. Aristotle, *Ethics* I.i). (Sidney's definition of *the* 'architectonic' art is (the Platonic) 'Know Thyself' as a responsible human being, both morally and socially.) The greatest good as pursued by this art, is not a mere

knowledge of what is good, but virtuous *action* (cf. 39.8–9n.). Conse-
quently—and Sidney could here be accused of begging the question—
the art most capable of stimulating virtuous action is the greatest art.
As Greville points out in his biography of Sidney, this doctrine
of knowing good and doing good was characteristic of Sidney's
attitude to life.

p. 29, l. 9. *next*, nearest.

p. 29, l. 10. *so*, similarly.

p. 29, l. 26 *definitions, divisions, and distinctions*. In scholastic
logic each question is qualified by an elaborate analysis ('division'
and 'distinction') of the number of parts contained in the terms
defined. Moral philosophy 'teacheth what virtue is' by taking it
through the traditional 'topics' or logical 'places' of invention (i.e.
the common distinctive marks of a thing), such as 'causes and effects',
opposites, agents, whole, parts, &c. The entire paragraph is, of course,
ironical.

p. 30, l. 9. *accord*, cause to agree.

p. 30, l. 14. *inquisitive of*, eager for.

p. 30, l. 15. *chafe*, temper.

p. 30, ll. 17–18. *testis* &c., [history is] 'the witness of times, light of
truth, life of memory, teacher of life, messenger of antiquity' (Cicero,
De Oratore II. ix).

p. 30, l. 19. *disputative*, fit for academic disputations.

p. 30, l. 22. *Marathon*, where in 490 B.C. the Athenians killed thou-
sands of Persian invaders.

Pharsalia, Pharsalos, where Caesar defeated Pompey in 48 B.C.

Poitiers, where the Black Prince captured John II, King of France,
in 1356.

Agincourt, the place of Henry V's remarkable victory over the
French in 1415.

p. 30, l. 31. *Brutus* (85–42 B.C.), who is said to have taken the history
of his ancestors for his guide.

p. 30, l. 32. *Alphonsus of Aragon* (1396–1458), a notable patron of
the arts with a special liking for Livy's histories, who is said to have
cured himself from sickness by studying the deeds of Alexander
the Great.

p. 31, ll. 3–4. *standeth for*, is put to judgement before.

p. 31, ll. 4–5. *moderator*, one who presides over an academic disputation.

p. 31, l. 16. *rather formidine* &c., rather through fear of punishment than for love of virtue. From Horace, *Epistles* I.xvi. 52–53: 'Oderunt peccare boni virtutis amore: Tu nihil admittes in te formidine pœnæ' ('The good hate vice because they love virtue: you [, slave,] will commit no crime because you dread punishment').

p. 31, l. 20. *him*, the lawyer.

p. 31, l. 22. *these*, the other three: poet, historian, and moral philosopher.

p. 31, l. 23. *naughtiness*, moral badness.

p. 31, l. 25. *manners*, moral conduct.

p. 32, l. 1. *wade in him*, go through the tedious task of reading his books.

p. 32, l. 7. *particular truth*, see 35.5 ff.

p. 32, l. 15. *an image*, or 'speaking picture' (cf. 25.18 and 33.2), conveys with brevity and force an entire concept which the philosopher's logic could only have defined circumstantially: 'shapes, colour', &c. (ll. 20–21 below). Cf. 29.26. n.

p. 32, l. 20. *exquisitely*, with uncommon exactness.

p. 32, l. 22. *architector*, architect.

p. 32, l. 32. *memory*, see 28.10 ff. n., and cf. 51.4–5 n. Without the visualizing aid of imagery, arguments cannot be retained in the memory and so become useless to one's 'judging power'.

p. 33, l. 5. *Anchises*, Aeneas' father (*Aeneid* II.638–49).

p. 33, l. 6. *Ulysses* and the nymph Calypso in *Odyssey* v.149–58.

p. 33, ll. 13–14. *genus and difference*, general concept and distinguishing marks.

p. 33, l. 15. *Ulysses* &c. The five epic examples given all belong to the history of Troy: *Diomedes*, King of Aetolia (e.g. *Iliad* VII.399 ff.; *Aeneid* II.162 ff.); *Nisus and Euryalus* (*Aeneid* v.294 ff.: IX.176 ff.), cf. 75.16.

p. 33, ll. 16–17. *an apparent shining*, an evident, visible brilliance.

p. 33, l. 19. *Atreus*, who served up his brother's children at a banquet prepared for his brother Thyestes.

p. 33, l. 20. *the two Theban brothers*, Eteocles and Polynices, who, having banished their blind father Oedipus, each desired to be only ruler of Thebes.

p. 33, l. 22. *Gnatho*, the parasite in Terence's *Eunuch; Pandar*, the go-between in Chaucer's *Troilus & Criseyde*.

p. 33, l. 24. *seats*, general shapes by which these virtues &c. may be remembered more easily. See 51.4–5 n.

p. 34, ll. 8–9. *Mediocribus* &c., '. . . but that poets be of middling rank, neither men nor gods nor booksellers ever brooked' (Horace, *Art* 372–3).

p. 34, l. 12. ff. *Christ* &c. The parables were often quoted as the final justification of 'poetic' teaching.

p. 34, l. 14. *Dives*, the rich man, in Luke xvi:19 ff.

p. 34, l. 16. *the lost child*, the prodigal son, in Luke xv: 11 ff.

p. 34, l. 23. *acts*, records.

p. 34, l. 29. *Aesop's tales*, for centuries every child's first reading book.

p. 34, l. 30. *formal tales of beasts*, only in form or outward appearance 'tales of beasts'.

p. 35, l. 6. *Aristotle*. Sidney quotes and paraphrases from *Poetics* ix a passage crucial to sixteenth-century poetic theory.

p. 35, ll. 7–8. φιλοσοφώτερον and σπουδαιότερον, philosophoteron and spoudaioteron.

p. 35, l. 10. καθόλου, katholou.

p. 35, l. 11. καθέκαστον, kathekaston.

p. 35, l. 25. *doctrinable*, instructive.

p. 35, l. 26. *Justin* (*fl.* A.D. 300?), author of excerpts from a (lost) world history by Trogus Pompeius.

p. 35, l. 27. *Dares Phrygius*, supposed author of a pretended eye-witness account of the Trojan War.

p. 35, l. 28. *fashion her countenance to the best grace*, have her face painted with the most becoming features.

p. 35, l. 30. *Canidia*, the witch in Horace, *Epodes* v, and *Satires* I.viii.

p. 35, ll. 32–33. *Tantalus*, Atreus' grandfather, who, among other things, served up his son at a banquet of the gods in order to try their omniscience. Punished in Hades, Tantalus may neither drink nor eat, although he is standing up to his chin in water and apples grow before his mouth.

p. 36, l. 3. *cannot . . . of* &c., is not at liberty (unless he resorts to poetic devices) to give &c.

p. 36, l. 4. *Alexander* the Great as described in Quintus Curtius Rufus' *History* (*c.* A.D. 50).

Scipio Africanus whose military and civil career is treated by Livy.

p. 36, ll. 10–11. *doth warrant . . . follow*, is a better guarantee for that which he must follow.

p. 36, l. 12. *that was*, that which was.

p. 36, l. 14. *a gross conceit*, an unrefined understanding.

p. 36, l. 15. *only informs a conjectured likelihood*, teaches, gives form to, that which may be conjectured to be likely, but no more.

p. 36, l. 16. *go by reason*, ignores reason.

him, i.e. the historian.

p. 36, l. 20. *fortune*, the vicissitude of things, which, being an irrational and unpredictable factor, makes nonsense of the examples of history and their use to posterity (cf. 37.25).

p. 36, l. 27. *Zopyrus*, in Herodotus, *History* III.153 ff.

p. 37, l. 1. *Tarquinius* Superbus and his son Sextus, in Livy, *Hist.* I. liii–liv.

p. 37, l. 3. *Abradatas*. Sidney confuses the King of Susa with one Araspas of whom Xenophon writes in *Cyropaedia* VI.i.39.

p. 37, l. 10. *faction*, intrigue.

p. 37, l. 15. *authority*. On the scope and authority of poetry cf. p. 24.

p. 37, l. 19. *to*, as to, in reply to.

p. 37, ll. 30–31. *the tragedy writer*, i.e. Euripides as quoted in Plutarch, *How to Study the Poets* 4.

p. 38, l. 1. *terror*, deterrent.

p. 38, l. 3. *Miltiades*, whose advice to the Athenians had resulted in the victorious battle of Marathon, soon found popular favour turning against him and died in an Athenian prison.

Phocion, the Athenian general who, like Socrates before him, was condemned to drink poison (318 B.C.).

p. 38, l. 5. *cruel Severus*, Lucius Septimius Severus (A.D. 146–211), Roman Emperor.

p. 38, ll. 5–6. *excellent Severus*, Marcus Aurelius Severus Alexander (A.D. 208–35), Roman Emperor, murdered by his own mutinous soldiers.

p. 38, l. 6. *Sulla*, Lucius Cornelius Sulla (138–78 B.C.), powerful Roman dictator and embittered opponent of Consul Caius *Marius* (156–86 B.C.).

p. 38, l. 7. *Pompey*, Gnaeus Pompeius (106–48 B.C.), Roman General, who was killed when seeking refuge in Egypt.

Cicero (106–43 B.C.) was murdered when trying to escape from Rome.

p. 38, l. 9. *Cato* the Younger (95–46 B.C.), who committed suicide after his party had failed to defeat Caesar (cf. 57.12).

p. 38, l. 10. *his name*, i.e. *caesar* meaning emperor (as in sixteenth-century Latin; and cf. German *Kaiser*).

p. 38, ll. 12–13. *who*, i.e. Caesar; *his*, i.e. Sulla's.

p. 38, l. 13. *literas nescivit*. Suetonius (*Life of Julius Caesar* 77) quotes Caesar who, playing on the word *dictatura* (i.e. both 'dictatorship' and 'dictation'), remarked when Sulla resigned as dictator that *Sullam nescisse litteras, qui dictaturam deposuerit*: 'that Sulla was ignorant of letters, since he left the *dictatura* to others'.

p. 38, l. 14. *by*, with reference to.

p. 38, l. 17. *occidendos esse*, 'that [tyrants] ought to be killed'. The topical subject of tyrannicide was being debated in print by some of Sidney's Protestant acquaintances.

p. 38, l. 18. ff. *Cypselus* and his son *Periander*, tyrants of Corinth (seventh century B.C.); *Phalaris*, tyrant of Agrigentum (fifth century B.C.), who used to roast his enemies alive in a brazen bull; *Dionysius* the Elder, tyrant of Syracuse (fourth century B.C.): all four were, historically speaking, able and successful statesmen, and the last three were notable patrons of the arts.

p. 38, l. 20. *kennel*, pack (of hounds).

p. 38, l. 22. *he*, i.e. poetry.

p. 38, ll. 23–24. *setting it forward*, inciting it.

p. 38, l. 28. *it may be questionable*, there may still be difference of opinion as to whether that which poetry teaches is better than the teachings of philosophers.

p. 39, l. 1. φιλοφιλόσοφος, philophilosophos, a philosopher's friend.

p. 39, l. 2. *moving*, or, in the classical tripartition of the orator's aims, 'persuading'—next to teaching and delighting. See 71.21 ff. n.

p. 39, ll. 8–9. *not* γνῶσις *but* πρᾶξις, not gnosis but praxis. '. . . τὸ τέλος ἐστὶν οὐ γνῶσις ἀλλὰ πρᾶξις', 'the end [of man's activities] is not to acquire understanding (knowledge) but to achieve things (action)' (Aristotle, *Ethics* I.iii). Cf. 29.5 ff.

p. 39, l. 18. *painfulness*, application, taking pains.

p. 39, l. 23. *a free desire*. Characteristically, Sidney blends the Platonic notion (cf. 41.20 and 47.12–13) that to recognize the good is to love it (and to love it is to desire to possess it) with a Protestant insistence on the power of 'the inward light'.

p. 39, l. 28. *natural conceit*, an understanding based on 'nature' (cf. 23.14–17), as against the scholastic terms ('words of art') through which they speak to us.

p. 39, l. 30. *hoc opus* &c. In *Aeneid* VI the Sibyl tells Aeneas that the gates of hell are open day and night, 'Sed revocare gradum superasque evadere ad auras, Hoc opus, hic labor est. Pauci, quos aequus amavit Juppiter aut ardens evexit ad aethera virtus, Dis geniti potuere': 'But to recall thy steps and pass out to the upper air, this is the task, this is the toil! Some few, whom kindly Jupiter has loved, or shining worth uplifted to heaven, sons of the gods, have prevailed' (128–31).

p. 39, l. 31. *human*, not divine sciences (cf. 31.10–14 ff).

p. 40, l. 5. *blur the margin*, i.e. surround the actual text with a mass of notes and commentary, like a learned treatise.

p. 40, l. 16. *aloes or rhabarbarum* (rhubarb), two bitter purgatives.

p. 40, ll. 26–27. *conveniency*, propriety.

p. 40, ll. 27–28. *as Aristotle saith*, in *Poetics* iv.

p. 40, l. 31. *Amadis de Gaule*, the Spanish romance which, in a French translation, became extremely popular in the sixteenth century. Various passages in Sidney's *Arcadia* derive from it.

p. 41, ll. 6–7. *Fugientem* &c. Turnus, Aeneas' great rival, in *Aeneid* XII. 645–6 speaks these prophetic lines to his sister: 'Terga dabo et Turnum fugientem' &c., 'shall I turn my back and shall this land see Turnus in flight? When it shall come to this, is it so sad to die?'

p. 41, l. 13. *masking raiment of poesy*, cf. 19.26 n.

p. 41, l. 15. *indulgere genio*, indulge in following their inclinations, as said by Luxuria in Persius' fifth satire: 'Indulge genio, carpamus dulcia, . . .' (151).

p. 41, ll. 18–19. *good-fellow*, boon companion, thief. Both meanings apply.

p. 41, l. 25. *Menenius Agrippa*. The story was first told in Livy, *Hist.* II.xxxii.

p. 41, l. 32. *geometry*. Over the door of Plato's Academy it was, supposedly, written that 'no man untaught in geometry should enter'.

p. 42, l. 11. *Nathan*, in 2 Sam.xii: 1–15.

p. 42, l. 17. *ungratefully*, cruelly.

p. 42, ll. 19–20. *the second . . . cause*, the first cause being God desiring him to be moved to repentance.

p. 42, l. 21. *psalm of mercy*, i.e. Psalm li.

p. 42, l. 28. *familiar*, suitable.

p. 43, l. 8. *Sannazzaro* (1458–1530), author of an influential pastoral work, *Arcadia*, to which Sidney is much indebted for his own *Arcadia*.

p. 43, l. 9. *heroical and pastoral*, e.g. Torquato Tasso in his *Gerusa-lemme Liberata* (1575).

p. 43, l. 16. *Pastoral*, traditionally the 'lowest' of the genres (cf. 27.11), although 'the poor [shepherd's] pipe' was made to treat some of the greatest themes in Elizabethan poetry.

p. 43, ll. 19–20. *Meliboeus*, a shepherd deprived of his property in Virgil's 1st eclogue; *Tityrus*, Virgil himself in shepherd's guise, rejoicing in the return of his possessions (ibid.).

p. 43, ll. 30–31. *Haec memini* &c., 'this I remember, and how Thyrsis, vanquished, strove in vain. From that day it is Corydon, Corydon with us' (Virgil, *Eclogues* VII.69–70). All that is left to posterity of Alexander's momentous victory over the Persian king (330 B.C.) is the trifling consideration that the one, like Corydon, won, and the other lost.

p. 43, l. 32. *lamenting Elegiac*. Sidney restricts the elegiac genre to complaint and reflective verse, and disregards all other forms of elegiac poetry.

p. 44, l. 1. *Heraclitus* of Ephesus (*c.* 500 B.C.), 'the weeping philosopher'.

p. 44, ll. 6–8. *Iambic*, from ἴαμβος, iamb, the iambic trimeter being first used by Greek writers for direct attack or exposure; as against the *Satiric* proper, which employs ironic methods of ridicule.

p. 44, ll. 9–13. *Omne vafer* &c. Said by Persius of the great satirist Horace, and condensed by Sidney from the original 'Omne vafer vitium ridenti Flaccus amico Tangit, et admissus circum praecordia ludit': 'While his friend laughs, sly [Quintus Horatius] Flaccus touches up his every fault, and, once admitted, can play with his very vitals' (*Satires* I.116–17).

p. 44, l. 16. *Est Ulubris* &c., the last lines of Horace, *Epistles* I.xi, adapted: '. . . petimus bene vivere. Quod petis hic est, Est Ulubris, animus si te non deficit aequus.' ('. . . We seek to make life happy. What you are seeking is here, it is at Ulubrae, if there fail you not a mind well balanced.') Ulubrae was an almost proverbially uninspiring town surrounded by marshes.

p. 44, l. 17 ff. *Comic.* Comedy, often a licentious form of entertainment, was rarely condemned so strongly as in late-sixteenth-century London (cf. 51.21 n.); but Sidney argues (54.5 ff.) that such plays are man's abuse of comedy, not the fault of comedy itself. He joins the majority of sixteenth-century theorists in giving a didactic justification of the genre: a. it ridicules folly, b. it teaches the straight by showing the crooked. The 'comedian' (i.e. 'comedy-writer', or possibly 'comic actor') must, therefore, clearly indicate by a 'signifying badge'—e.g. 'typical' dress, looks, behaviour—the general folly of a comic character in order to show 'who be such' and so stress the moral point.

p. 44, l. 31. *Demea*, the father in Terence's *Adelphi*.
Davus, a servant in Terence's *Andria*.

p. 45, l. 1. *Thraso*, the bragging soldier in Terence's *Eunuch*.

p. 45, l. 7. *pistrinum*, in Roman times the pounding mill, normally worked by asses, where slaves could be sent for punishment: cf. Terence, *Andria* I.ii.28, '. . . te in pistrinum, Dave, dedam usque ad necem'.

p. 45, l. 8. *the sack*, as in Aesop's fable (Phaedrus IV.10) of the two bags, one filled with one's own faults and carried on the back, there to be seen by others and not by oneself.

p. 45, l. 15. ff. *Tragedy*, together with the epic, both being great in scope and manner, was subjected to endless theoretical discussions throughout the Renaissance and after. Sidney's only, but important, departure from the main (Aristotelian) line of argument is in calling the 'affects' (emotions) stirred by tragedy 'admiration' (great wonder and reverence) and 'commiseration', instead of 'pity and fear'. 'Fear' itself he reserves for the royal spectator (l. 17), or he relegates it to the tragic theme, as in the couplet 'Qui sceptra &c.'. 'Who harshly wields the sceptre with tyrannic sway, fears those who fear: terror recoils upon its author's head' (Seneca, *Oedipus* 705-6).

p. 45, l. 25. *Alexander*, the cruel tyrant of Pherae, wept at the sufferings of Hecuba and Andromache when seeing Euripides' *Troades* performed (Plutarch, *Life of Pelopidas* 29).

p. 46, l. 4. *Lyric*. Sidney elaborates the formal definition of this 'part', viz. poetry chiefly of praise and (originally) sung with musical accompaniment.

p. 46, l. 7. *natural problems*, discussions of questions of natural philosophy.

p. 46, l. 10. *Percy and Douglas*, the ballad of *Chevy Chase*.

p. 46, l. 11. *a trumpet*, the instrument of (actual) battle.

p. 46, l. 12. *crowder*, fiddler.

p. 46, l. 16. *Pindar* (c. 520-440 B.C.), the great Greek lyric poet, of whose works only the *Epinicia*, hymns in praise of Olympic victors, survive.

Hungary. In the summer of 1573 Sidney visited Hungary, which was then largely occupied by the Turks (cf. 20.21 n.), before travelling from Vienna to Italy.

p. 46, l. 20. *Lacedemonians*. The manner in which martial songs were sung by the three age-groups of Spartan men is described in Plutarch's *Life of Lycurgus* 21.

p. 46, l. 30. *toys*, trifles.

p. 46, ll. 31-32. *Philip of Macedon*, Alexander the Great's father, who on one day received three great tidings: that his general had been victorious in an important battle, that his horse had won the race at

Olympia (Sidney mistakenly writes 'Olympus'), and that his wife had borne him a son, Alexander.

p. 47, l. 3. *Heroical*, or epic, which Sidney, in agreement with traditional views, considers to be the greatest form of poetry (27.10–11).

p. 47, l. 7. *Tydeus*, one of the seven heroes who fought against Thebes, in Statius' *Thebais*.

Rinaldo, Orlando's cousin in Ariosto's *Orlando Furioso*; or, more probably, the noble captor of Jerusalem in Tasso's *Gerusalemme Liberata*.

p. 47, l. 23. *be worn … memory*, be constantly available as an inspiring example, indelibly inscribed in one's memory (cf. 51.4–5n.).

p. 47, l. 26. *ceremonies*, sacred objects.

p. 48, l. 4. *melius Chrysippo* &c. In *Epistles* I.ii, Horace argues that Homer is a better guide for students of moral philosophy than even Chrysippus (third century B.C.), the great Stoic, or the Platonist Crantor (*fl.* 300 B.C.).

p. 48, l. 12. ff. *Since then* &c. Before answering certain specific accusations (especially 51.21 ff.), Sidney here gives a careful summary of all his preceding arguments in praise of poetry.

p. 49, l. 12. μισόμουσοι, misomousoi, from μισο- (of μισεῖν, to hate) and μοῦσα, Muse, with masc. pl. ending -οι; perhaps Sidney's own coining.

p. 49, l. 16. *spleen*, regarded as the seat of laughter.

p. 49, l. 23. ff. *the discretion* &c. Formal eulogies on jocose subjects were common (cf. 17.24–25 n.). The German scholar Cornelius Agrippa in his *De Vanitate Scientiarum* (1530) praised 'the discretion of an ass'; Francesco Berni (1497–1535) eulogized, among other things, both 'being in debt' and 'being sick of the plague'; and Erasmus praised folly in his *Moriae Encomium* (1511), *The Praise of Folly*.

Ovid, in *Ars Amatoria* II.661–2, suggested that a woman who is too small should not be called *brevis* (short) but *habilis* (nimble, pleasantly light), 'et lateat vitium proximitate boni' ('and thus a fault will "lie hid in nearness of" a virtue')—which Sidney here, in his turn, parodies.

p. 50, l. 10. *already said*, viz. in 27.15 ff.

p. 50, l. 14. *Scaliger*, in *Poetices* I.ii, states that the 'poet' is in the first place a 'maker of verse'.

p. 50, ll. 15–16. *oratio next to ratio*, a classical commonplace to distinguish man from animal.

p. 50, l. 19. *forcible quality*, accent (cf. 73.11).

p. 50, l. 21. *without*, unless.

p. 50, l. 24. *music*. In the sixteenth century the reasons why (and the ways in which) music had an irresistible effect upon its hearers were subjected to much learned speculation and analysis. In the present context music is important since it aids the poet in 'moving' his listeners (cf. 38.29 ff.; and 73.8 ff. n.).

p. 50, l. 33. *accusing itself*, betraying itself.

p. 51, ll. 4–5. *the art of memory*, the art of remembering facts or arguments, commonly by forming images of each fact or part of argument in association with a 'locality', for instance in a 'room' 'well and thoroughly known'. These localities—'natural seats' (cf. 33.24 n.)—have much in common with the *loci* ('places' or 'topics') of logic and rhetoric (see 28.10 ff. n. and 29.26 n.).

p. 51, l. 17. *compiled in verses*. Throughout the Middle Ages, and after, much basic school knowledge was taught, and memorized, in rhymes.

p. 51, l. 21. *imputations*. From a wealth of traditional attacks on the moral and social usefulness of poetry, Sidney here selects four of the best-known charges. The third in particular had recently been publicized in *The School of Abuse* (1579), which its author, Stephen Gosson, had thought fit to dedicate to Sidney. Some of the latter's *Defence* may be read as a reply to Gosson. Thomas Lodge answered Gosson in an essay also known as *Defence of Poetry* (1579).

p. 51, ll. 29–30. *as Chaucer saith*, viz. 'I have, God woot, a large feeld to ere' (*Knight's Tale* 28), suggesting—though without reference to comedy—that a long story must be cut short. 'To ear' is 'to plough'.

p. 52, l. 7. *petere principium*, beg the question.

p. 52, l. 18. *liars*. The notion that poets, because they deal with fiction, must be liars is repeated, and refuted, monotonously from antiquity onwards.

p. 52, l. 25. *Charon*, the ferryman of the Underworld.

p. 52, l. 33. *circles*, within which only, as in witchcraft, a spell can operate.

p. 53, l. 3. *entry*, the opening lines in which the Muses are invoked.

p. 53, l. 8. *before-alleged*, viz. in 42.11 ff.

p. 53, l. 10. *Aesop*, see 34.30 ff.

p. 53, ll. 22–23. *an imaginative ground-plot*, a foundation, itself built by the imagination, and 'profitable' to the reader as a firm basis for his own 'inventions'.

p. 53, ll. 27–28. *John-a-stiles and John-a-nokes*, originally 'John (who dwells) at the stile' and 'John (who dwells) at the oak', fictitious names traditionally used for the two parties in a legal action.

p. 54, ll. 29–30. εἰκαστική, eikastike, making likenesses; φανταστική, phantastike, making fantasies. The distinction was made by Plato (*Sophist* 36).

p. 54, l. 31. *fancy*, the delusive imagination.

p. 55, l. 14. *conceiveth his title*, receives its rights, its justification.

p. 55, l. 15. *rampire*, rampart, defence.

p. 56, l. 2. *Albion*, suggesting the remotest history of England even before the name Britain was introduced (cf. 20.33).

p. 56, l. 4. *chainshot*, two cannon balls connected by a chain.

p. 56, l. 5. *certain Goths*. The anecdote—relating to the sack of Rome —is given in the continuation of Dio Cassius' *Roman Histories* (ed. U. P. Boissevain, 1901, III, app. 3, 169).

p. 56, l. 7. *hangman*, meaning also 'villain' in a more general sense.

p. 56, l. 21. *jubeo* &c., 'I bid him be a fool as much as he likes', Sidney's adaptation from Horace's 'Quid facias illi? iubeas miserum esse libenter' (*Satires* I.i.63).

p. 56, l. 23. *poetry is the companion of camps*, a sixteenth-century commonplace, much repeated within Sidney's literary milieu, and exemplified in Sidney himself.

p. 56, ll. 25–26. *the quiddity . . . materia*, 'the essence of being and first matter', a 'typical instance' of scholastic jargon.

p. 56, l. 32. *motions*, prompting.

p. 57, l. 1. ff. *Alexander's example*. Plutarch wrote of Alexander's

virtues, and described how the King never travelled without his copy
of the *Iliad* ('dead Homer'), which he used to keep under his pillow,
with his sword. *Callisthenes* was a relation of Aristotle, who went to
Asia with Alexander.

p. 57, l. 12 ff. *Cato* Maior (234–149 B.C.), the Censor, stern critic of
everything Greek. *Cato Uticensis* (see 38.9 n.) was his great-
grandson. M. *Fulvius* Nobilior, made Consul in 189 B.C., took
Ennius (239–169 B.C.) with him when campaigning in Greece.

p. 57, l. 17. *the former*, i.e. Cato Maior.

p. 57, l. 24. *unmustered*, not formally enrolled in the army.

he misliked not. Strictly speaking: he need not therefore have
misliked.

p. 57, l. 25. *Scipio Nasica*, P. Cornelius Scipio Nasica, who, judged
to be the best citizen of Rome, was chosen by the Senate to fulfil
certain commandments of the oracle in 204 B.C.

p. 57, l. 26. *the other Scipio brothers*, the one surnamed Africanus for
his victory over Hannibal in 202 B.C., the other Asiaticus for his
victory over Antiochus in 190 B.C., both patrons of Ennius.

p. 57, l. 32. *Plato's name.* Sidney now deals with the notorious
accusations against poetry in Plato, *Republic* ii and x.

p. 58, ll. 2–3. *the most poetical*, cf. 19.25 ff., and 41.11 ff.

p. 58, l. 17. *seven cities*, viz. Argos, Athens, Chios, Colophon,
Rhodes, Salamis, and Smyrna.

p. 58, ll. 20–21. *had their lives saved*, as related in Plutarch's *Life of
Nicias* 29.

p. 58, l. 22. *unworthy to live*, e.g. Socrates, condemned to drink
poison (399 B.C.).

p. 58, l. 23. *Simonides* of Ceos (556–468 B.C.), lyric poet, one of
the writers patronized by *Hiero* I, tyrant of Syracuse (478–467
B.C.).

p. 58, l. 26. *was made a slave*, by the Spartan ambassador to whom
Dionysius (see 38.18 ff. n.) is said to have given him.

p. 58, l. 27. *do thus*, viz. argue in this unfair manner.

p. 58, l. 28. *cavillations*, seemingly clever repartees.

p. 58, ll. 31–32. *and see . . . they do.* Sidney follows Scaliger and
others in charging Plato with homosexual tendencies.

p. 59, l. 1. *community of women*, in *Republic* v.

p. 59, ll. 9–10. *twice citeth* &c. The poets referred to are Aratus (third century B.C.) in Acts xvii:28, and Epimenides (fifth century B.C.) in Titus i:12. Olney's edition, without marginal note, reads: '... allegeth twice two poets'. The editor may have thought in addition of Menander (fourth century B.C.) quoted in 1 Cor. xv: 35, and of Cleanthes (333–231 B.C.) whom Acts xvii: 28 may also echo.

p. 59, ll. 10–11. *a watchword upon philosophy*, a word of warning against philosophy: 'Beware lest any man spoil you through philosophy . . .' (Col. ii:8).

p. 59, l. 22. *Plutarch*, in his *Morals*.

p. 59, ll. 31–32. *Qua authoritate* &c., 'which authority certain barbarians and uncivilized persons seek to misuse in order to have poets banned from the state' (*Poetices* i.ii).

p. 60, l. 1. *law*, indulgence, a sporting term meaning the allowance in time or distance made to an animal that is to be hunted.

p. 60, l. 10. *lion's skin*, as in the fable of the ass, who, wishing to seem a lion, crept into a lion's skin.

p. 60, ll. 14–15. *more than myself do*. Sidney deviates from the main trend in sixteenth-century poetics by denying that the source of poetic genius is some sort of 'divine' inspiration (ἐνθουσιασμός). His own views are given on pp. 24–25. (cf. also 75.6–8).

p. 60, l. 21. *Laelius*, friend of the Scipios, by some thought to have assisted Terence in the writing of *Heautontimorumenos* (i.e. 'self-tormentor', ἑαυτὸν τιμωρούμενος)'

p. 60, l. 25. *the only wise man*, according to the oracle of Delphi (Plato, *Apology* xxi). In prison Socrates versified some of Aesop's fables (Plato, *Phaedo* lx).

p. 60, l. 30. *Plutarch*, in his *Morals*.

p. 60, l. 33. *guards*, ornamental trimmings.

p. 61, l. 18. *run a career*, run a gallop at full speed before coming to a sudden stop.

p. 61, l. 25. *Musa* &c., 'tell me, o Muse, the cause: which offence to the deity?', from Virgil's invocation (*Aeneid* 1.8).

p. 61, l. 28. *Adrian*, P. Aelius Hadrianus, Roman Emperor (A.D. 117–38), author of some poetry.

Sophocles (496–406 B.C.), the Greek dramatist, in 440 B.C. appointed one of the ten generals in the war against Samos.

Germanicus Gaius Iulius Caesar (15 B.C.–A.D. 19), commander of the Roman troops against the Germans, who wrote several poems.

p. 61, l. 30. *Robert* II of Anjou, King of Sicily (1309–43), a poet, and patron of Petrarch.

p. 62, l. 1. *King Francis* I (1494–1547), a great patron of scholars and artists.

p. 62. l. 1. *King James*, probably James I (1394–1437), author of *The Kingis Quhair*.

p. 62, l. 2. *Bembus*, Cardinal Pietro Bembo (1470–1547), famous for his neo-Latin poetry.

Bibbiena, Bernardo Dovizi (1470–1520), Cardinal of Bibbiena, humanist and author of one comedy.

p. 62, l. 3. *Beza*, Théodore de Bèze (1519–1605), French philologist and, after the death of Calvin in 1564, leader of the Calvinists; author of various literary works.

Melanchthon, Philip Melanchthon (1497–1563), German humanist-poet, the influential supporter of Luther.

p. 62, l. 4. *Fracastorius*, Girolamo Fracastorio (1483–1553), natural philosopher, author of a well-known medical poem.

Scaliger, Julius Caesar Scaliger (1484–1558), humanist-poet, author of *Poetices* which inspired various passages in Sidney's *Defence*.

Pontanus, Giovanni Pontano (1426–1503), diplomatist, author of widely esteemed works on a variety of subjects.

p. 62, l. 5. *Muretus*, Marc-Antoine Muret (1526–85), humanist-poet, renowned for his elegant Latin style.

Buchanan, George Buchanan (1506–82), Scottish humanist, eminent neo-Latin poet (cf. 69.16), closely connected with Sidney's circle.

p. 62, l. 6. *Hospital*, Michel de l'Hôpital (1505–73), Chancellor of France, advocated toleration and encouraged the arts, author of a number of Latin poems.

p. 62, l. 18. *strew the house*, cover the floor with rushes, prepare a welcome.

p. 62, l. 19. *the mountebanks at Venice*, the notoriously voluble quacks of sixteenth-century Venice.

p. 62, l. 21. *like Venus*, who was caught (in adultery with Mars) in a net made by her husband Vulcan (Homer, *Odyssey* VIII.266–366). Poetry, Sidney suggests, would be capable of shaking the Englishman's lethargy.

p. 62, l. 24. *grateful to idle England*, agreeable to England at peace. Sidney was a known opponent to England's neutral foreign policy

p. 62, l. 28. *Epaminondas* (d. 362 B.C.), the general to whom Thebes owed its temporary supremacy in Greece, and who, according to Plutarch, gave dignity to the previously contemptible office of a telearch.

p. 63, l. 2. *Helicon*, the Boeotian mountain, often confused with Hippocrene, the fountain of the Muses on Mount Helicon, which was said to owe its existence to the imprint of Pegasus' hoof.

p. 63, l. 3. *post-horses*, horses used in relay by postriders, or kept for hire.

p. 63, l. 5. *Queis meliore* &c. 'whose hearts the Titan [Prometheus] has made of better clay', adapted from Juvenal, *Satires* XIV.35, where the line refers to the rare youths who will not be corrupted by the bad example of their elders.

p. 63, l.12. *in despite of Pallas*, or *invita Minerva*, against Minerva's will, i.e. without talent.

p. 63, l. 19. *look*, behold, examine.

p. 63, l. 27. *orator* &c., 'an orator is made, a poet born', a post-classical proverbial saying.

p. 63, l. 29. *manured*, cultivated.

Daedalus (δαίδαλος, wrought by art), the mythological inventor and wise technician who, having constructed artificial wings for himself and his son Icarus, in vain advised the latter not to fly too near the sun or his waxen wings would melt.

p. 64, l. 3. *fore-backwardly*, starting at the wrong end.

p. 64, l. 9. *quodlibet*, 'anything we like', any question proposed for exercise (in academic disputation).

p. 64, l. 11. *Quicquid conabor* &c. Sidney adapts Ovid's verse 'Et quod conabar dicere, versus erat' (*Tristia* IV.x.26) to mean: 'Whatever I shall try to say, it will turn into verse'.

p. 64, l. 19. *Mirror of Magistrates*, the *Mirror for Magistrates* (1559

etc.), a collection of poems by various writers, including Thomas
Sackville (1563 ed.) on the downfalls of illustrious English statesmen.

p. 64, l. 20. *Surrey's lyrics*, the poems by Henry Howard, Earl of
Surrey (1517?–47), printed in *Songs and Sonnets* (the so-called *Tottel's
Miscellany*) of 1557.

p. 64, l. 22. *Shepherds' Calendar* (1579), Spenser's first major
publication, dedicated to Sidney.

p. 64, l. 24 ff. *That same framing* &c. Sidney does not dare to 'allow'
(i.e. approve of) Spenser's consciously rustic and archaic language in
the *Shepherds' Calendar* because the three great pastoral authors did
not 'affect' it: Theocritus (third century B.C.), writer of *Idylls*;
Virgil in his *Eclogues*; and Sannazzaro (see 43.8 n.). Note, however,
that in Sidney's own *Arcadia* eclogues there is much 'old rustic
language', too.

p. 65, l. 1. *tingling*, tinkling.

p. 65, ll. 3–5. *Our tragedies* &c., nominative absolute construction.

p. 65, l. 4. *honest civility*, decency.

p. 65, l. 5. *Gorboduc*, the tragedy of the warring British princes
Ferrex and Porrex, by Thomas Sackville and Thomas Norton, first
acted (before Queen Elizabeth) in 1561, the first English tragedy in
blank verse.

p. 65, ll. 16–17. *Aristotle's precept* &c. In *Poetics* v, Aristotle observed
that in a tragedy the action does not normally exceed in time 'one
revolution of the sun'. On the unity of action—i.e. that everything
in a play should contribute to one main action—he laid great stress;
but the unity of place—a corollary dictated by 'common reason'—
was a term invented by Renaissance critics. Together the 'three
unities', then codified, were to play a major part in seventeenth-
century dramatic theory.

p. 65, l. 18. *inartificially*, not in accordance with true art.

p. 66, l. 9. *matter of two days*. The reference to *Eunuch*, in which the
action does not exceed one day, must be a mistake.

p. 66, l. 12. *in one place*, viz. in *Captives* where the rule of time is not
observed.

p. 66, l. 25. *Pacolet's horse*, the magic horse of the dwarf Pacolet in the popular French romance of Valentine and Orson, first printed in English in the middle of the sixteenth century.

p. 66, l. 26. *Nuntius*, Messenger.

p. 66, l. 28. *ab ovo*, 'from the egg'. Horace (*Art* 147) remarked that the good poet would not write about the Trojan war 'from the twin eggs' (out of one of which Helen was born), but would rush the reader *in medias res*, 'to the principal point of action'.

p. 66, l. 32 ff. *Polydorus* &c. The story is that of Euripides' *Hecuba*.

p. 67, l. 17. *decency*, appropriateness.

p. 67, ll. 18–19. *neither . . . sportfulness*, neither the aims of tragedy (cf. 45.15 ff. n.) nor of comedy.

p. 67, l. 20. *Apuleius* (second century A.D.), author of *Metamorphoses* (known as *The Golden Ass*).

p. 67, l. 23. *Amphitryo*, which Plautus himself called a 'tragicocomoedia'.

p. 67, l. 30. *tract*, extent.

p. 68, l. 6. *conveniency*, agreement, similarity.

p. 68, ll. 18–19. *go . . . bias*, end in unexpected disaster, as when in the game of bowls a slope will divert the bowl from a proper course according to its bias.

p. 68, ll. 19–20. *for the respect of them*, on their account.

p. 68, l. 24. *mad antics*, grotesque representations.

p. 68, l. 25. *Hercules*, who, when infatuated with the Queen of Lydia, Omphale, was subjected to this humiliating reversal of roles.

p. 69, l. 1. *Aristotle*, in *Poetics* v.

p. 69, ll. 9–10. *Nil habet* &c., 'of all the woes of luckless poverty none is harder to endure than this, that it exposes men to ridicule' (Juvenal, *Satires* III.152–53).

p. 69, l. 14. *naturally*, in actual life.

p. 69, l. 15. *in the other*, viz. in tragedy.

p. 69, l. 18. *they*, i.e. comedy and tragedy .

p. 70, l. 8. *energia* (ἐνέργεια), the proper degree of force of expression.

p. 70, l. 14. *affectation*, pretence (cf. *Astrophil and Stella* xv).

p. 70, l. 17. *coursing of a letter*, hunting letters, e.g. in alliteration.

p. 70, ll. 18–19. *figures and flowers*, figures of speech and choice phrases.

p. 70, ll. 25–26. *Tully and Demosthenes*, invariably quoted as the models of eloquence.

p. 70, l. 27. *Nizolian paper-books*, notebooks full of phrases, like the *Thesaurus Ciceronianus* (1535) compiled by the Italian Marius Nizolius. In 1578 one of Sidney's acquaintances, Henri Estienne, had written and published *Nizoliodidascalus* to stop the evil influences of Nizolian Ciceronianism, as he explained in a prefatory letter to Sidney's friend and teacher Hubert Languet.

p. 70, l. 28. *attentive translation*, studious transference.

p. 71, l. 3. *Vivit. Vivit? Imo* [vero etiam] *in senatum venit*, '. . . he lives. Lives? Why, he even comes into the Senate!' (from the opening of Cicero's first *Oratio in Catilinam*).

p. 71, l. 8. *familiar epistle*, letter to a friend.

p. 71, l. 9. *choler*, a pun on 'colour' (ornament of style).

similiter cadences, or *similiter cadentia*, the ending of words with the same cases or the ending of clauses with similar syllables, as in excessively rhythmic pseudo-Ciceronian oratory such as Sidney criticizes throughout this passage.

p. 71, l. 11. *daintiness*, good taste.

p. 71, ll. 17, 18. *finesse*, artistic subtlety.

p. 71, l. 18. *similitudes*, similes, with special reference to the 'Euphuistic' practice of employing abundance of comparisons with plants, animals, &c., as in John Lyly's very popular *Euphues* (1578).

p. 71, l. 21 ff. *conceits*. Sidney, 'straying from poetry to oratory' (72.15–16), here indicates both the connexion and the differences between rhetoric and that which he calls 'poetry' but which his contemporaries—especially those who were influenced by the French scholar Petrus Ramus—would have termed 'logic' or 'dialectic'. Rhetoric, which may be divided into eloquence (tropes and figures) and delivery, aims at winning 'credit' (Lat. *fides*) in order to 'persuade' (l. 32 ff; and cf. 39.2). The other art, the art of arguing well, has three divisions: 'conceit' (or *inventio*), 'judgement' (or *dispositio*), and 'memory' (cf. 28.10 ff. n.). It aims at enlarging and purifying the understanding by establishing truths. Sidney does not divorce rhetoric from that other art, but stresses the function of logically suitable 'oratory'—*viz.* 'persuasion' or moving (cf. 39.2 n.)—for

cf p85

what he looks upon as 'poetry'; and implies that true poesy is both dialectic and rhetoric.

p. 71, l. 29. *Antonius and Crassus*, speakers in Cicero's *De Oratore*.

p. 72, l. 1. *mark*, aim.

p. 72, l. 5. *curiously*, exquisitely.

p. 72, l. 15. *pounded*, shut up in a pound like an animal gone astray.

p. 72, ll. 16–17. *in the wordish consideration*, where words, or 'diction', are concerned.

p. 72, l. 28. *both the other*, probably refers to Anglo-Saxon and French.

p. 73, l. 5. *compositions*, i.e. compounds, of which numerous instances may be found in Sidney's own works: e.g. 'self-wise-seeming' (69.12), 'honey-flowing' (70.12–13; from Lat. *melli-fluus*), '*μισόμουσοι*' (49.12).

p. 73, l. 8. ff. *versifying*. In the sixteenth century—in England especially in the 1570s and 1580s, and earlier in France—the merits of the two ways of versifying, *viz.*, quantitative verse *or* verse (generally rhymed) according to number of syllables and/or number of accents, were much debated, and Sidney himself composed numerous experiments. Discussions invariably centred upon the presupposed connexion between poetry and music (cf. 50.24 n.); and it was often felt that quantitative verse has the greatest affinity with music because both observe 'time' (long/short) or duration.

p. 73, l. 15. *time*. Some editions read 'tune', but 'time' was probably intended. Cf. the cancelled passage in *Arcadia*, where one speaker puts forward that in a happy combination of quantitative verse and music the verse-feet 'as it were kindly accompany the time' (Sidney, *Poems*, ed. W. Ringler, Oxford, 1962, p. 390); and cf. 23.13.

p. 73, l. 16. *express diverse passions*, cf. 30.16 n.

p. 73, l. 21 ff. *Truly the English* &c. After a long period in which the learned poets and courtiers had been inclined to minimize the relative value of vernacular composition, Sidney's generation again recognized and proclaimed the merits of their native language. This paragraph, and the preceding one, herald, as it were, the spectacular recovery of English literature during the second half of Queen Elizabeth's reign.

p. 73, l. 25. *Dutch*. In Sidney's time 'Dutch' referred to the languages both of Germany—a language Sidney is known to have disliked—and of the Low Countries. His remark could apply in either case.

p. 73, l. 31. *rhyme*, as against 'the very rhyme itself' (see 74.3), is accentual verse generally.

p. 74, l. 7. *sdrucciola*, 'slippery', when the last stressed syllable is followed by more than one unstressed syllable. 'Motion: potion' (line 12) Sidney regards as a trisyllabic (*sdrucciola*) rhyme.

p. 74, l. 27. *Aristotle*. Not in Aristotle, but as in Boccacio, *Genealogia Deorum* xv.8: '. . . eosque primos fuisse theologizantes testatur Aristotiles.'

p. 74, l. 29. *Scaliger*, in *Poetices* III.xix (cf. 33.27 ff).

p. 74, l. 32. *Clauserus*, i.e. the German Conrad Clauser, in the preface to his translation *De Natura Deorum* (1543) of Θεωρία περὶ τῆς τῶν θεῶν φύσεως by the Stoic pedagogue L. Annaeus Cornutus (first century A.D.).

p. 75, l. 3. *quid non*, what not.

p. 75, l. 6. *Landino*, the Florentine humanist Cristoforo Landino (1424–1504) in the prologue to his edition of the *Divina Commedia* (1481), cf. 60.14–15 n.

p. 75, l. 14. *libertino patre natus*, 'a freedman's son', as Horace called himself in *Epistles* I.xx.20 and *Satires* I.vi.6, 45, 46.

p. 75, l. 15. *Herculea proles*, 'the offspring of Hercules'.

p. 75, l. 16. *Si quid* &c., 'if aught my verses avail [no day shall ever blot you from the memory of time]' (Virgil, *Aeneid* IX.446, with reference to the undying memory of the dead warriors Nisus and Euryalus (cf. 33.15 n.)).

p. 75, ll. 17–18. *your soul* &c., i.e. in Paradise or the Elysian fields.

p. 75, ll. 19–20. *cataract of Nilus* &c. It was commonly believed that those who lived near the roaring waterfalls of the Nile had lost all sense of hearing (cf. Cicero, *Dream of Scipio* 5). Earthbound men, Sidney is saying, are insensitive to poetry, which, like the music of the spheres, cannot be heard by dull minds.

p. 75, l. 23. *such a mome as to be a Momus*, such a fool as to be a fault-finder like Momus (μῶμος, ridicule), the son of Night and Sleep, the god of ridicule and captious criticism.

p. 75, l. 24. *Midas*, the Phrygian king who (in Ovid, *Metamorphoses* XI) was given the ears of an ass because he judged the music of Pan to be superior to that of Apollo.

p. 75, l. 25. *Bubonax*. In Pliny, *Natural History* XXXVI.5.4, the sculptor Bupalus, who had portrayed the ugly poet Hipponax, is said to have been driven to suicide by the latter's satirical verses.

p. 75, l. 26. *rhymed to death*, by means of rhymed charms such as the Irish were said to use against rats.

INDEX OF NAMES